Here's What Peo

"In *Step Up, Step Out,* author Carolyn Hart shares her four-year journey from wounded to gifted, from victim to liberator. Beyond the pain of pursuing the 'American Dream' there is an awakening that happens when Carolyn follows her calling to be an agent of change. You'll meet a who's who of transformational agents, and ultimately yourself, on this international trip through impermanence, the fullness of emptiness, and the stages of the healing process."

> —Donny Epstein, DC; author, *12 Stages of Healing, Healing Myths, Healing Magic: Breaking the Spell of Old Illusions; Reclaiming Our Power to Heal;* developer Network Spinal Analysis, SomatoRespiratory Integration, Reorganizational Healing and Living. www.donaldepstein.com

"Given the dedication, effectiveness, and leadership role Carolyn has taken in her stand for an environmentally sustainable, spiritually fulfilling, and socially just human presence, I feel certain that Carolyn's book and documentation of her journey will be a great contribution to the world we all dream of."

> —Lynne Twist, founder and president, Soul of Money Institute, www.soulofmoney.org; cofounder, The Pachamama Alliance, www.pachamama.org

"Every now and then, a book comes along with the right message at just the right time. As small effects in one part of a system can lead to big changes in another, doing your own personal growth work contributes to planetary evolution. *Step Up, Step Out* details the journey of a woman I know well. Her determination to regain wholeness not only transformed her life, but contributed to everyone she touched along the way. Leading by example, her story demonstrates what is possible for everyone."

> —Dr. Sherri Tenpenny, founder, Tenpenny Integrative Medical Center; author, *Saying No to Vaccines: A Resource Guide for All Ages*; contributing author, *Vaccine Epidemic: How Corporate Greed, Biased Science, and Coercive Government Threaten Our Human Rights, Our Health, and Our Children*

"*Step Up, Step Out* is a heartwarming book that highlights why doing your personal growth work is essential at this critical time in history. Carolyn Rose Hart takes you on a journey of healing and shows you how, collectively, we really can make a difference for the future of humanity."

—**Christine Kloser,** publisher, *Pebbles in the Pond: Transforming the World One Person at a Time;* www.christinekloser.com

"Carolyn Hart is spontaneous, courageous, and inspiringly humble as she embarks on a four-year international odyssey where she also can no longer avoid facing repressed childhood abuse. She beautifully recounts her inner and outer travels with heart and sincerity as she strives to truly see the other, whether an indigenous tribesman in Ecuador or the perpetrators of her past, and live her purpose in every word, deed, and decision. *Step Up, Step Out* is an inspiring read and a guide to clear the past and risk and live the authentic life."

—**Cynthia Gonzalez,** author; speaker; seminar leader

"In her introduction, Carolyn Rose Hart asks, 'Have you shared your gifts with the world?' In *Step Up, Step Out: Share Your Gifts and Be an Agent for Change,* she does just that. Whether you are an adventurous soul or dream of taking a journey to wellness, this book is for you. Carolyn courageously shares the wisdom, personal dance, and education she embraces in exchange for sharing her gifts, not as a tourist but as a global human being in Ecuador, Bali, Uganda, and beyond. She vividly describes and exemplifies the life skills she has developed in a world setting."

—**Kimberly Burnham, PhD;** author, *The Nerve Whisperer: Recover Your Life Through Brain Health*

"If you've overcome emotional and physical abuse to successfully enjoy a rewarding career and family life, but still felt something deeper was missing—take a read of Carolyn's heartfelt journey where she steps up and steps out to discover purpose, passion, and what's truly precious to us all."

—**Carolyn Hidalgo, CPCC;** relationship coach; consultant; author, *Live the Love You Deserve: How to Surrender Criticism & Practice Non-Judgment to Experience Eternal Love*

"I just finished Carolyn Rose Hart's *Step Up, Step Out* and feel like I have truly experienced the richness of this global journey, the inner harmony of a spiritual retreat, and the optimism of Hart's view of Global Oneness. Her journey of personal healing was like that pebble in the pond sending healing ripples to so many others who encountered this amazing woman. For all 'adventurous souls who are standing on the precipice,' jump! Join Hart as she gently leads us upon our own soul-searching, global, healing journey. I am better for having read this book."

> —**Ann White,** transformational author, *Living with Spirit Energy: Bring Balance and Harmony into Your Life and World*

"This is an engaging story of a woman's journey to wholeness. After retiring from the teaching profession, Carolyn Hart traveled the world and found personal healing and empowerment. Her amazing courage and tenacity guided her to a transformed life—one of greater awareness, new energy, and a new career. She is currently training facilitators in programs on the Journey of the Universe: Awakening the Dreamer."

> —**Kay Eaton and CeCe Miller,** cofounders, Sacred Space, Cleveland; www.sacredspacecleveland.org

"A book for all courageous souls who find the lingering pain of their past stopping their gifts from shining. Carolyn shares the hope for your life to make a difference as you set the intention to clear the residue and open to incredible possibilities. I am excited for the change and growth that happens in the lives of those who read this book."

> —**Daniel Knowles, DC;** clinician; researcher; speaker; Board of Trustees for Sherman College of Chiropractic; www.networkwellnesscenters.com

"*Step Up, Step Out* is an inspiring personal chronicle that has much to offer us in our collective evolution of global consciousness. Enjoy an evening with Carolyn as she imparts with candor and courage her story of transformation—from victim to a woman of vision who is making a difference for all life on this planet. A must-read."

> —**Mary Southard CSJ;** artist; www.marysouthardart.org

"Words in this book touched me so deeply. Carolyn Rose Hart gives voice to all who have struggled to find peace in themselves due to love deprivation. She paves the way on how to claim love back into oneself regardless of what others have done to us. Her bravery, not just to explore the world in search of love, but more importantly to explore deeply inside herself and find it, is exemplary. Her courage to answer her calling gave her back her heart. With the scent of roses exuding continuously from her loving heart, reading her story, we find she is indeed the Courageous Rose Heart."

—**Dr. Rose GS**; The Message Is Love; www.drrosegs.com

"*Step Up, Step Out* is a brilliant example of the power of sharing vulnerably of personal pain and the journey to awareness, and inspiring others to contribute to a just and sustainable world."

—**Ken Stone,** The Soul Archaeologist; internationally recognized teacher and healer; www.KenWStone.com

"In *Step Up, Step Out*, Carolyn Hart repeatedly confronts us with the challenge of 'doing our personal work' and from hindsight, invites us along with her on the journey of doing her personal work down to the bone. Her courage in revealing so much that was painful, puzzling, terrifying, and ecstatically liberating in her journey is the same courage that allowed her to dive deep into the wounds that many of us prefer to keep hidden or pretend do not exist. At this point in her history, she proclaims that she wants nothing more than to be an agent for planet-altering change and invites us to do the same. But becoming a change agent is far more than a proclamation: It is an irreversible commitment to the Wounded Healer in all of us—the only source of authentic transformation. Carolyn Hart has painstakingly lived this metamorphosis, and I urge you to read her book."

—**Carolyn Baker, PhD**; author, Navigating the Coming Chaos: A Handbook for Inner Transition

Step Up, Step Out

Share Your Gifts and Be an Agent for Change

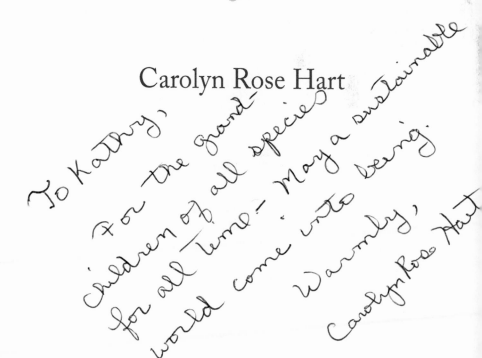

Carolyn Rose Hart

To Kathy,

For the grand-children of all species for all time— May a sustainable world come into being.

Warmly,
Carolyn Rose Hart

Spiritwise Publishing
Boulder, Colorado

Spiritwise Publishing,
PO Box 93
Boulder, CO 80306
720-306-1255
or Spiritwise59@gmail.com.

Printed in the U.S.A.
First printing 2012

ISBN: 978-0-615-61799-2
LCCN: 2012905120

Interior layout by VortexDesign.biz
Editing by Kate Deubert
Cover Design: Graphic by Manjari
Cover Photo: Barbara Pettibone

ATTENTION CORPORATIONS, UNIVERSITIES, COLLEGES, AND PROFESSIONAL ORGANIZATIONS: Quantity discounts are available on bulk purchases of this book for educational, gift purposes, or as premiums for increasing magazine subscriptions or renewals. Special books or book excerpts can also be created to fit specific needs. For information, please contact

Spiritwise Publishing,
PO Box 93
Boulder, CO 80306
720-306-1255
or Spiritwise59@gmail.com.

To my children, Tom and Melissa...
Thank you for your patience, support, and love while I
confronted my four-year journey.
Most of all, thank you for being my teachers.
I have learned so much from you about myself.

Acknowledgments

I wish to offer my earnest thanks to:

My family, for contracting with me in this lifetime to teach me the lessons I came to learn. And for your love.

Jaclyn Miller, Ph.D., for being my teacher extraordinaire. Without you, I would still be doubting myself and feeling, "I'm not good enough."

My Aunt Helen, who unselfishly released me from taking care of her so I could do what was for me to do at this time in history.

The residents of the Village at St. Edward Independent Living, who shared so many dinners with me and expressed curiosity about where I was and what I was up to.

My brother, Joe; my sisters, Allison and Lauren; and my nephews, Kevin and Blake, who remained connected to me and always interested, asking, "Where in the world is Carolyn now?"

Barbara Starre and Kathy Quintus, for their encouragement and grounding in the importance of my journey.

Bill, for his devotion in listening to my stories and viewing thousands of photos.

Carol Dombrose and all my housemates at Angel House Strongsville, for putting up with my crotchety demeanor when I returned to Cleveland for brief respites.

Kate Deubert, for her phenomenal editing skills and clarity about my journey, and for giving me so much to ponder about my story.

Christine Kloser, the transformational catalyst. Without you, my book would still be in my head and my heart.

The open and giving people around the world who invited me into their loving homes as I traveled.

All those who babysat my car when I flew to a new destination.

The many people who supported my journey, my process of clearing my past abuse, and my writing. I appreciate you all.

Itinerary

Introduction

"I realized that family patterns live on not just in behaviors. They live on in patterns of thought. They live through a certain acquiescence, a belief that things never change so you must go along in order to get along."
—IYANLA VANZANT

If you knew you had only four years to live, what would you do with the precious time you had left? Would you remain angry or would you forgive all those who have wronged you? Would you apologize to anyone you may have harmed? Would you travel to the exotic place you've always dreamed of? What is your purpose in life and have you fulfilled that purpose? Have you shared your gifts with the world? What are your gifts? Have you trusted yourself, reached out, acted boldly, switched the switch, and *stepped out* into your dreams? What are your dreams? Would four years be enough time to live into those dreams?

After retiring from teaching with my children grown and flown, I realized the American Dream was no longer my dream. As I became even clearer about my deep longing for more, I sold my 2,200 square foot home with a huge kitchen, two-and-a-half bathrooms, living room, dining room, family room, four bedrooms including my exercise and meditation room, a huge office with floor-to-ceiling bookshelves, a first-floor laundry room, two-car attached garage, front porch with feng shui fountain, and a rear patio with hot tub, all situated on a beautifully wooded lot. I also sold 80 percent of a thirty-year accumulation of stuff. What really *is* the American Dream?

This release of things was freeing—and scary. Some of my family and friends found it to be horrifying. Yet, I asked, "What was the purpose of all this stuff in my life, anyway?" Those who were just on the precipice of the so-called American Dream had obvious difficulty comprehending my path.

Throughout my childhood and early adult life, I was deeply aware of the physical, sexual, and mental abuse that occurred in my formative years. Yet, as one of the courageous, strong beings in my family of ten siblings, I always chose the high road. As a single parent of two beautiful children, I worked full time and attended graduate school for my master's degree in education. What was I going to do now that I had retired and my children were on their own? Where was I going to live now that I had sold my house and most of its contents? The former abuse rose to fill the space, challenging me to face it, finally.

Life is incredibly complex and there is a "knowing" in the Quantum Field. James Allen, Professor of Physics at UC Santa Barbara says, "You are today where your thoughts have brought you. You will be tomorrow where your thoughts take you." In quantum science we are creating the results in our daily lives through every word we allow in our monkey mind. Learning to pay closer attention to my thoughts was a valuable lesson on my road to recovery. I was now the headmistress of my future.

I meditated, journaled, danced, chanted, and processed in an attempt to dive into the pain and clear it once and for all. The wombat in me would not let me give up on the dream of being free of my past abuse, urging me to *step up* and share my gifts and truly be the person I was meant to be.

"What is the significance of my life?" "What is my life's purpose?"

"How do I evolve to my highest being and clear my past?" I had a knowing that living in an apartment or condo in Cleveland, Ohio, would not answer these questions at the deep level I was seeking. Given my strong passion for adventure and an intense desire to connect with other people, I set out on an expedition. I would not rent or buy a place to live. I would travel for a year and live out of my car. That one year turned into four.

There is a difference between group travel, tourism, and immersion with the locals. Coming from a teaching background assisting challenged learners in the classroom, I found myself a quasi expert at reading illegible handwriting, deciphering unintelligible speech, and decoding body language. I had developed an expertise in distinct pronunciation of words so my students could follow my instruction and learn to read and write. With these techniques under my belt, the country folk where I was traveling loved talking with me. They would say, "I can understand your English. You pronounce your words very distinctly." I did not need to know ten languages to navigate different cultures and ways of life. Negotiating a new country became a dance for me. It was about connection and immersion rather than tourism. I sought out ways to live in communities with people from all over the world and partake of programs offering new ways of getting at core issues that were stopping me from being all I could be.

As I traveled the world, many of my friends told me, "You have to write a book." This book is my attempt to share my process and my newfound gifts for others to wade through, ponder, and *step up* to their own best self. It is intended for those adventurous souls who are standing on the precipice with matters of contention to be released. Once you let go of these issues, the space for expressing your best self will become apparent. This is my gentle nudge for those wanting to *step up* and *step out*.

The world is in an Evolutionary Shift. Barbara Marx Hubbard says we are becoming a "Universal Humanity," connected and awakened from within to express and to be more. Personal work is crucial, a necessary segue into the collective shift. Since we are the ones we have been waiting for, now is the time for each individual to make the shift. Each person has a part to play that comprises a piece of the whole. It is in the collective that the world will move to a more conscious level but this shift depends on individuals. Each of us must do the work if the collective is to make the shift.

I would like to invite you to experiment with the many suggested exercises and activities that you will find in this book. If they work for you on your personal path, fantastic! Take what you like and leave the rest. Each person will find a way to wholeness and what works for them. In finding their wholeness, individuals will be ready to *step up* and *step out*.

I would like to invite you, also, to join me on my continuing journey to wholeness by visiting my website: www.CarolynRoseHart.com. Join me on my blog or follow me on Facebook at https://www.facebook.com/StepUpStepOutBook and Tweet with me at https://twitter.com/#!/StepupStepoutbk. Connecting in community is the new paradigm and this community can be in person, through teleconferencing, blogging, tweeting, and through supporting and learning more about each other. More heads are better than one. Together we can create amazing things. I look forward to sharing our future on behalf of all the generations to come.

PART I

A Soul Having a Human Experience

(pictured on previous page) A view of downtown Cleveland, Ohio from the Cuyahoga River. The Terminal Tower and The Federal Courthouse Tower can be seen along with one of the many bridges in The City of Bridges.

CHAPTER 1

Uncover the Muck

*"The intuitive mind is a sacred gift
and the rational mind is a faithful
servant. We have created a society that
honors the servant and has forgotten
the gift."*
—ALBERT EINSTEIN

In the modern world, or eagle way of life, we tend to live in our head while the condor societies are more spiritually oriented and live by opening their heart and honoring nature. The prophecy of the eagle and the condor says that we are at a time in the history of mankind that the condor will fly in the same skies as the eagle and the world will come into balance. The indigenous cultures, the condor societies, are sharing this prophecy with the people in developed countries and are indicating a whole new future is possible. By integrating these two worldviews incredible possibilities open up for all life on this planet.

Imagine spending the first half of your life aligning your mind with your heart and purpose in life. I was totally living in my head as I pursued survival in a family of eleven children with an abusive, alcoholic, paranoid-schizophrenic father and a depressed mother. Growing up in a dysfunctional home kept me vigilant, doubtful, and cut off from my feelings. I was always in my head trying to figure out life and control everything and everyone, because my life was out of control.

I was born a Condor and I know my purpose in life is to open my heart to all that is and love all life on this planet. This purpose of opening the heart and loving nature was moved aside through the abuse in my formative years and my need to stay alert and protective of my body. I was to clear deeper issues and prepare myself for the Evolutionary Story or, as the late Thomas Berry calls it, "The Great Story." As well, Sr. Mary Southard in a *Spiritearth Publication* says, "We will begin to do what humans do best: Be amazed! Be filled with reverence! Contemplate! Fall in Love! Be entranced by the wonder of the Universe, the uniqueness of each being, the beauty of creation, its new revelation each day, and the Divine Presence within all!"

So, when one stays in one's head, what gets pushed aside? Feelings. I now know that feelings are a huge part of the human experience. Throughout the day, I will ask myself this question, "How does that make me feel?" Through asking and answering, I keep the channels of my feeling self open and aware, unlike when I was a child and young adult.

Oh, the secrets behind closed doors. If you had asked me ten years ago, "How does that make you feel?" I probably would have taken out a sheet of smiley faces and shown you which one matched what was inside me. I was that disconnected from my feelings. If someone told me I couldn't do something, I would go on a mission, gritting my teeth all the way, to prove them and the world wrong. Because I embodied fear of judgment and blame, I judged and blamed. I became a doubting Thomas, even questioning if my grandmother was truly my grandmother. You see, my older brothers told me she was just an old woman that my uncle felt sorry for and took into his home.

I lacked trust. I never knew if something behind me was lurking to attack my being. I became very good at building compensatory skills and ways to protect myself. I would escape the real world through daydreams of the good life. I would blame myself if something went wrong and try even harder to make it work—one way or another. That is the effect of secrets behind closed doors. The stiffness, tenacity, and perfectionism in my life created a rigidity, holding back the spontaneous sweetness of life. I found myself working, working, working, and ultimately depleting my energy and health.

My evolutionary story does not surprise me. It seems inevitable that I was the first one in my family to graduate with a master's degree and accumulate sixty-seven additional hours in the education arena. Furthermore, as a single parent, I achieved buying a lovely sprawling home and filled it with beautiful stuff in order to give my two children all the advantages. Then I was able to retire in my early fifties, staying busy to prove to myself that I was still a success. I am sure people who knew me wanted to say to me, "I can't hear what you're saying over all that you're doing." I had to protect myself from the feelings that knocked on my door when I was not busy.

Not having spoken many words until the age of five, I found it difficult to open the doors of life to access feelings. Feelings are the avenue to the heart and the way of the Condor people. As a sexual abuser, my father closed down everything that stirred in my body. This devout Catholic little girl became even more confused. Escapism was the only way to survive. I believe my mother knew what was going on behind closed doors. She had a rule, "What goes on in this house, stays in this house." Even my mother was a victim. We were all victims—all thirteen of us. The tribal energy was sick.

I escaped this madness through stuffing my feelings, by not trusting anyone, including myself, and by working hard. Determined to avoid alcoholism, I gritted my teeth all the way to workaholism. In our culture, workaholism is a respectable addiction, one that I came to realize is just as addictive and harmful as any other. Of course, our society would define me as a success. After all, I had a good job, a house in the suburbs, two beautiful children, and took vacations. I want to share with you that this is not success.

The traditional American Dream erodes the American people. A good deal of my four-year journey confirmed for me that the American Dream also undermines other societies and devalues the lives of people all over the world. Traveling to Uganda opened my eyes to just how much stuff we have, and still we are not happy. To make our cell phones, we mine the metal tantalum—a $6 billion industry—in rebel countries such as the Democratic Republic of the Congo, thus funding violent outbreaks. When we seek out a new cell phone every two years, we contribute to the erosion of civilizations around the world. This has a direct link to human rights abuses and I am choosing not to be part of this insanity of getting a new phone every two years anymore.

Another eye-opener occurred when I traveled to the Amazon in Ecuador. It became clear to me that our national love of the automobile and our driver-only commutes contribute big-time to the eroding of the rainforest. We continually seek different venues to drill for oil, leaving a path of destruction in the homelands of people who have lived there for generations. Without the rainforest, the Lungs of our Planet will be gone, along with 20 percent of the Earth's oxygen. The indigenous people of the Amazon are our keepers of these beautiful lands where ten million species of plants, animals, and insects live. As protectors of their environment, they are the Condor people.

We are also destroying our own environment. Some recent instances are the oil leak in Yellowstone National Park, the oil spill in the Gulf of Mexico, fracking or injecting highly-pressurized fluid to find the hard-to-get oil, and the Keystone XL pipeline that will travel 2,147 miles from Canada to the Gulf Coast all in the name of obtaining more oil. These and many more examples have impressed on me what is happening to Mother Earth and have strongly influenced my becoming whole and healthy. Julia Butterfly Hill says it so eloquently, "We cannot have peace on the Earth until we have peace with the Earth."

Approximately 75 percent of our behaviors are unconscious behaviors. What if we focused our attention on the 25 percent that are conscious behaviors and opened up to the possibility of 45 or 65 percent consciousness? What if we made better decisions for ourselves and all life on this planet? Opening to the world and sharing what I have learned is crucial for me as a moral human being. If we as a society do not know and understand how we have an impact on other living beings, we will stay unconscious. We are all connected. We are all one.

My journey around our country and around the world has truly been a heart opener. I have embraced my feelings and clarified my purpose in life. I am also clearer about what I must do at this time of our Evolutionary Shift.

CHAPTER 2

In a Fog

*"People generally see what they look
for, and hear what they listen for."*
—HARPER LEE, *TO KILL A
MOCKINGBIRD*

Imagine sharing your travels with eighty- and ninety-year-young women who refer to you as a "vagabond." Whenever I returned to Cleveland, I would spend a day or two visiting with my aunt. We went shopping, fixed issues in her apartment, and always ended the day at dinner in the dining room of the independent living facility in which she resides. The friends she tootles around with, especially at dinnertime, would delight in calling me a vagabond or wanderer. They truly loved hearing my travel stories and flipping through my photos. Likewise I enjoyed hearing their travel stories and seeing pictures of their families. What a treat to be in their wisdom energy of giving and taking.

What will it take to close the doors of our institutional houses for the elderly and physically move them back into society where they can share their incredible wisdom? As I peel the layers of my former encasement, I begin to question the structure of our institutions. The people of the Amazon don't put their elderly away. The generations in a family live together sharing physically, mentally, and emotionally. These aha moments are precious to me.

I refer to myself as a "woman of the world." By tapping into my inner child, I have continually opened doors on my journey. By traveling solo and putting myself out there, I found a universe open up to me. I was amazed at the number of women who were literally traveling just as I was, exploring all the world has to offer. Incidentally, now that I am rooted in an apartment, I no longer bump up against other women of the world. How interestingly energy works. A person's energy will match another like energy allowing the two energies to come together and create amazing things.

Energy also spirals out into the dark night. My intention evolved into clearing my past and brought the peeling of the onion layers right into my lap. I wanted to wash my skin to cleanse my soul. These two things—travel and clearings—informed one another in the energy field. They would be my alchemy of life, opening me up to the sweet surrender of all things possible in the world. It would be like a serpent shedding its skin. I was on an expedition to discover my true self, but I did not realize it, at first.

What if I allowed my dragons to keep me small? Dragons such as shame, fear, or guilt. What if I chose not to push through what was scary, not to take my unsatisfying life to a satisfying life? This was not part of my story. I consciously live with the knowing that whenever I have the option to try something new, I will take it. Magical things happen when I follow what the Universe presents me with.

I am an adventurer, so, without much nudging and prodding, I set out on the road to exploring. Carl Jung referred to the opposite natures in every human being as "masculine" and "feminine." My fully developed, protective, masculine side had served its purpose. Like a serpent sheds its skin, I would shed this perfectionist, competitive, analytical side of me by exploring any and all ways to expose and embody my feminine side. This would be my bliss.

CHAPTER 3

Question All That Is

*"When you change the way you look at
things, the things you look at change."*
—DR. WAYNE DYER

The late Ted Andrews in his book, *Animal Speak*, says, "The bear teaches us to go in and awaken the potentials inherent, the tree serves as a reminder that we must bring what we awaken out into the world and apply it—make our marks with it."

In the first month of my four-year journey, I woke up at Sufi camp one morning with something rubbing up against my tent. I began pushing on the side of the tent to nudge what I thought was the free-range cow I'd seen the night before. Warm and cozy in my sleeping bag, I did not want to climb out to open the flap. The animal soon left. Later that morning, a friend who was camping across the road from me told me a bear had come close to her tent then wandered over to mine. The bear had been awakening my potential! It was in that moment that I knew my sojourn was going to be a spiritual journey.

Evolution occurs over time, but time has sped up here in the third millennium. As I immersed myself in meditation techniques, chanting, dancing, process work, Gestalt psychology, and massage therapy, among many other deeply moving experiences, time would slow down and I would feel the feelings. Attempting to process all that I was experiencing and all that was coming up for me was challenging. The brain, including my own, is socially programmed to see things in a certain way. I was meeting people from all over the world whose culture taught them differently from mine, and my sojourn was opening my eyes to other perspectives. I had been seeing an exquisite holistic psychologist, Dr. Jaclyn Miller, who would always remind me to listen to my feelings and encouraged me to write about what I was experiencing especially with my emotions. Journaling became my best friend.

As a living, breathing soul having a human experience, I often found myself "in my story." It was all about me. I learned to use my voice to open my memory. I would get angry or vengeful as I acknowledged the things that had happened to me. I now feel fortunate that I was uncovering all that was. Some individuals never completely encounter the ills that happened to them. The pain is intensely deep. For all of us, we may reach a point where it has served its purpose.

What do I mean by "served its purpose"? Shocking revelations change the experience of one's life, challenging the person to see beyond themselves. It gives them the opportunity to look at life in a deeper way. Knowing everything is energy and recognizing that the astral body, separate from the physical body, is connected to the nervous system, helps me to comprehend my experience as a reflection of what is happening with all of life. As a species, many of us have closed ourselves to the beauty of life and have sought to conquer, control, and appear better than our fellow human beings. At last, having gone into the pain and completed my "work," I can now intuit my formative years as serving a purpose for the understanding of what is happening to Mother Earth.

There is a great new story occurring now. A story that is absolutely essential in changing the mindset of human beings. Everyone and everything is a mirror of the self. We are one and I am enough. There is a power in me that no one can take away. It is exemplified by the Dalai Lama in his nonviolent ways, even in the face of extreme aggression. The Dalai Lama shows us what is possible through forgiveness and love.

So, I have come to see that opening up to all possibilities—and there are many—gives me hope. There is more to life than an organized closet. The more I accumulate, the less I experience life. I have gone from a 2,200 square foot home to a 350 square foot apartment and I have everything I need.

I felt as though I had reached a threshold of the hero's journey, where everything known is left behind, and I was venturing into an unknown realm where rules and limits are yet to be revealed. I was to learn many things on the journey but one of the most important was, "Everything is energy." If everything is connected and everything is energy, then what happens when an earthquake and a tsunami hit Japan? We are affected also. This learning was huge for me.

How did we as a species get to this place in history? Why do we assume some people are better and more deserving than others? How did we come to see all that Mother Earth offers as merely a resource for our taking? How did we decide it is our right to conquer nature and that animals do not feel, giving us the prerogative to treat them cruelly? Do we not experience this energy as we eat for our energy? My current choice of eating vegetarian several times a week is augmented with choosing sustainable meats. Sustainable meats for me are animals that have been treated humanely while alive, been humanely killed, and that have been fed no genetically modified organisms (GMOs), no pesticides or herbicides, and no antibiotics or hormones. Additives are not healthy for me or for the animals that are given these substances. Whenever possible, I choose pasture-raised and organic. I have reduced my consumption of meat to two or three times a week knowing this reduction is beneficial to the environment, my health, and the animals that give of themselves so that I may be nourished.

How did I come to adopt these principles in light of my

workaholism? I know my four-year journey impacted my values and morals, all the while opening my eyes to other ways of seeing the world. My journey continues to keep me in wonderment and a space of questioning all that is.

PART II

A Shift Occurs

(pictured on previous page) Crazy Horse, a Lakota war leader is depicted on this memorial in the Black Hills of South Dakota. It was initiated by the late Korczak Ziolkowski in 1948 honoring the culture and traditions of North American Indians. I was blessed to be in attendance for Korczak's wife's 80th birthday celebration with a spectacular nighttime blasting of the memorial. It was truly a special opportunity due to being in the right place at the right time.

CHAPTER 4

We Are All Connected

"Map out your future, but do it in pencil."
—JON BON JOVI

When I left Cleveland, Ohio, on June 16, 2006, it was my fifty-fourth birthday. Birthdays, literally, never meant a lot to me. As a child, if I became excited about my birthday, I may not have gotten any acknowledgment until evening. No one wished me "Happy Birthday" most years until the cake was brought out after dinner, and then I went to bed. I grew to have no expectations. As an adult, I learned to care for myself, so now I choose to do something special to honor this blessed day of mine.

I am a soul having a human experience. I am not the things I have or what I have accomplished. I started my expedition to grow and evolve by facing the joys, the lessons, the fears, and the dark side. So, leaving on my journey and following my bliss was truly honoring my special day. I did not know the Universe had big plans for me and conspired with me from the very start.

As the housing market began its descent in 2006, I prepared for a long journey of selling my house. Since I aspire to be a spiritual person with a consciousness that all possibilities exist, I cleared my home of negative energy by drumming, burning sage, applying feng shui, meditating, and most of all planting a statue of St. Joseph upside down on the property line as my Catholic friends had told me to do. The phone rang and broke my meditation. My realtor indicated that the young couple who had seen my house the week before would like to return for a second showing. It took them only a week to secure a loan, approve the home inspection, and for all of us—buyers and seller—to sign on the bottom line. This was just three weeks after listing my home.

Having expected the process to take nine-to-twelve months, I was now faced with decisions of where to live and what to do with my excess stuff. With my children grown and on their own, I could not decide if I wanted to buy a smaller house or a condominium, or maybe rent. What kept coming up for me was my passion for travel. I made the decision not to root, but instead to use the mortgage, insurance, and utility payments to follow my passion for travel.

What remained was releasing the burden of my possessions. What would I sell? What was precious enough to pay for storage? What would I need in my car on the road? What would I like to give away? Decisions, decisions, decisions. In less than two months, I completed this process—and process it was. I loaded up my 10-by-10-foot storage unit and packed my car. My burning desire to experience all things around the world was calling me.

How would I say good-bye to precious family and friends? Those closest to me posed a special kind of challenge. However, the day my eighty-nine-year-old aunt released me by telling me, "Don't stay for me. I can take care of myself. You go do what you need to do," would be a day filled with relief. She is a special person in my life and I am only a phone call away. I experienced three weeks of lunches, dinners, parties, etc. Somehow I, and everyone else, knew I would not return to live in Cleveland. There were tears shed as I said my good-byes knowing I would always be a Clevelander at heart.

My first experience was a travel writing class at the University of Iowa's Writing Festival. Being small is not part of my journey. Below, I would like to share with you my culminating writing project.

A Meeting of Two Souls

Many freeway miles had passed with more miles ahead for a 2000 Honda Accord and a fifty-four-year-old body. I had sold my home in Parma, Ohio, and would begin traveling to known and unknown parts within the United States. Pico Iyer stated, "Travel spins us around in two ways at once. It shows us the sight and values and issues that we might ordinarily ignore; but it also, and more deeply shows us all the parts of ourselves that might otherwise grow rusty."

This portion of my trip would bring me to the University of Iowa's 2006 Summer Writing Festival in Iowa City, Iowa. As I chose to take a break from the monotonous highway driving, I found myself in another rest area. The familiar rectangular building with a picnic area of metal tables, artificial cement trash cans, and towering trees added to the stark experience on Interstate 80 from west of Cleveland to Indiana.

Out of my peripheral vision, I could see her approach as I washed my hands with the sweet-smelling water and antibacterial liquid soap. The odor of cleanser was mixed with Calvin Klein's Obsession perfume belonging to a nearby traveler at the adjacent sink. A warm breeze blew through the open window of the women's turnpike restroom while the recently ingested taste of mixed nuts swirled in my mouth.

I could hear her mumbling amidst the flushing commodes and singing robins in the cherry blossom tree outside the open window. She was fiftyish, crouched over with a strange gait and a barely audible voice. She continued to proudly hold with her awkward hands a medal, which hung boldly around her gaunt neck. Its ribbon matched the colors of the American flag.

"Wfher errdss esdndn ende," she said.

"Oh! That's marvelous," I said.

"Rehdn enns oensend ei," she continued to murmur as she approached me.

I remarked, "I am so proud of you. It is very impressive."

"Wfher errdss esdndn ende," she said, once again.

I continued to respond, "You must have worked so hard to have earned such a brilliant medal. What an accomplishment."

She stared downward at the shiny linoleum tile then glanced upward into my eyes with a pride in the otherwise barren sockets of her face. The Olympic torch and five rings were apparent; yet, it was the gaze when two souls meet in the moment that remains with me today. As she shared her accomplishment, I knew this gift bestowed upon me in a public restroom was as precious as gold. The beauty of this timeless interaction stilled the sounds of people talking in the distance and water spraying from faucets.

The sight of this physically and cognitively challenged human being invokes issues that are waning and slowly rusting for me as I travel further from the profession of special education teacher that enveloped most of my adult life prior to retirement. It is clear to me that my travels are spinning me around in two ways at once, as Pico Iyer stated in his book, Salon Travel. I have opened my eyes to the precious resources available to travelers as I sojourn throughout this country, for this is what feeds my soul.

The Iowa Writing Festival was magnificent, fulfilling, and it gave me a sense that I could become an author. Upon leaving the university I traveled west to Sioux Falls, which has done wondrous things with their falls area. It was an odd feeling to be away from the university, my home, all that I knew. I immersed myself immediately into taking pictures, thus staying busy to keep the feelings at bay.

CHAPTER 5

Peeling the Outer Layers of the Onion

(Iowa to New Mexico)

"Everyone has been made for some particular work, and the desire for that work has been put in every heart."
—MOWLANA JALALUDDIN RUMI

Further west, I visited the Badlands, stopping at the famous Wall Drug, then on to the Black Hills where I experienced wild burros and American bison blocking traffic as they came out of the mountains. I immersed myself in this exquisite experience, connecting emotionally to other living beings, in a state of excitement for all that was new to me. I was alert enough to keep my windows raised and took photos through the windshield. When two adolescent bison came running toward my car expressing rutting behavior, I held tight to my seat praying they would not run into my car and damage it. They did not and it was a sweet experience.

I had always wanted to see Mount Rushmore. Carved into the granite face of the mountain are sixty-foot busts of four presidents, George Washington, Thomas Jefferson, Theodore Roosevelt, and Abraham Lincoln. I found myself in awe of the people who had crafted our nation's Shrine of Democracy. Socrates once said, "I know that I am intelligent because I know that I know nothing." I was viewing this magnificent monument from shaded eyes. There was no representation of the native people of our land who were pushed aside so that the white man could build the American Dream.

In contrast, as I visited Crazy Horse Memorial, still in the carving stages, I found myself becoming more conscious of what really occurred in our country. This monument commemorates the Sioux chief who refused to stay corralled on a reservation. I was completely awed into realizing there is another story that is being told. That night there was a twenty-minute commemoration for Ruth Ziolkowski's birthday. She is the president, chief executive, and wife of the late Korczak Ziolkowski, the monument's first sculptor. Honoring the culture, tradition, and living heritage of North American Indians through this monument is expansive and heart-warming for me. It is the honorable thing to do, yet, the monument is being carved by a private foundation, not the people of the United States. I so want to acknowledge this Crazy Horse Memorial Foundation.

Driving through Fort Collins initiated me to the genuinely friendly people of Colorado. It felt like home since the people living in the Midwest are likewise open and friendly. Estes Park was next. It is not for the meek and mild motorist but it is a glorious excursion in one very special national park. Elk roam on the open prairies high in the mountains, moving to lower elevations in the fall as the bull elk bugle for their mates. I live in deep appreciation for those who came before me and had the wherewithal to set aside such unique lands for future generations to enjoy. Currently, I am saddened and discouraged as our government downsizes the land our forebears preserved. We can make a difference by letting the government know how precious these lands are by emailing, faxing, and texting our concerns to our congresspersons.

Driving further south into Boulder, Colorado, placed me right in the middle of a community that has an air all its own. Bicyclists and pedestrians have the right-of-way at the many crossings throughout this quaint city. The diversity of things to do and places to go for a day is amazing. I discovered a Dances of Universal Peace Community of like-minded people during my weekend stay and would return to this city many times on my journey. Several months later on a return trip, I joined the Boulder Cruiser Ride. As I tooled around town one Thursday evening with more than two hundred students and adults in costumes, riding decorated bikes, I couldn't help but feel elated to be part of this ride. What a hoot!

Due to fatigue, I bypassed Manitou Springs and the Garden of the Gods, which are two of my favorite jaunts, and continued south toward my current destination, Sufi camp. After I had put more than two thousand miles on my car, the realization struck me that I was simply tired of driving. I started to take my sweet old time driving three-to-five hours a day the remainder of the way, stopping around 3:00 to check into a hotel. It was a holiday weekend and hotels that normally booked up by 9:00 P.M. would be filling up by 5:00 P.M. I had not reserved hotel rooms in advance, to allow myself the freedom of exploring as situations arose. I preferred to travel without restrictions and time constraints. It was the best way to seize the moment.

Traveling the back roads to Taos, New Mexico, eventually brought me to an exquisite restaurant, La Café Mystica, which will stay in my book of great places to experience while in the area. Later that day I stayed at a hotel in Taos that was the place to be and be seen. I was yearning for more connection at this point in my journey. Although I didn't realize it at the time, I was processing all that had occurred in the last few months: selling my beautiful home and its contents, and saying good-bye to longtime friends and family. With the encouragement of Jaclyn, my therapist, I allowed myself to experience sadness, regret, and loneliness, and to really feel these feelings. I was beginning to learn that the feelings would pass if I identified, felt, journaled, and allowed myself to process them. I was on a journey to clear and get healthy, but I still didn't know it at this point. I thought I was just exploring my passion for travel.

The Sufi Foundation of America Camp in New Mexico would be like returning home for me. I had spent time at this camp living in natural settings and nurturing myself, which provided an inner shift combined with an outer shift. My most exquisite experiences revolved around chanting and scarf dancing. The space I was able to move into provided a meditative experience, allowing me to clear my mind of clutter. While sitting out on the kitchen patio at camp one day after about four weeks of meditation, nature hiking, dancing, chanting, etc., I realized I did not have any thoughts. Not only had I lost ten pounds eating the vegan diet the camp served, but I had also cleared my chatterbox.

People from all over the world come to New Mexico to do the "work" of Adnan Sarhan, which gives the camp an international feel. I loved connecting with friends from past camp experiences and with new friends who had different perspectives on life. I found that we all want the same things: good health, good food and water, safety and happiness for ourselves and our families. We are all one. We are all connected.

On Tuesdays, our day off from camp, I often found myself with a group of friends visiting Chimayo, a church built over the sight of a miracle, soaking in the revitalizing mineral pools at Ojo Caliente, and stopping in Santa Fe to eat at Café Pasqual's, one of our favorites. I learned much about living in community while at Sufi camp. Give-and-take, sharing, doing my fair share—all are necessary facets of living with other people peacefully. Most of all, processing issues as they come up is crucial. I see our future as one of more community living. Are we ready to share and deeply communicate? Do we need all the "stuff" or can we live together with the give-and-take that supplies everyone with what they need rather than what they want?

I left Sufi camp in early September and began my journey to Big Sur, California. I took my time along the way to take in more sights around the country before entering our long coastal state. Roswell, New Mexico, with its alien museum and Cloudcroft where I treated myself to a suite at The Lodge, 9,000 feet above sea level, were my first stops. Tent camping had taken a toll on me.

Days later, a visit to Carlsbad Caverns and then Kartchner Caverns in Arizona gave me a new perspective on another unexamined assumption in our world. Caverns are living, breathing entities. We have just about ended the life of Carlsbad by exposing it to lint, open air, and a gazillion bodies walking through every year. In contrast, the "live" Kartchner Caverns are being conserved by limiting what enters the cavern and continually closing it so that water can percolate from the surface, forming the stalactites and stalagmites that have been growing for tens of thousands of years. Why wouldn't we want to protect this beauty?

Continuing west across the southern portion of Arizona, I visited Nogales, Mexico, and Biosphere 2 in Tucson. I had studied in high school about the Biosphere and the twelve people immersed for one year in this glass house. It was fun to explore and envision being one of them. My venture, thus far, began to show me that nothing is static in our world. Everything is continuously in motion and constantly changing. The Biosphere was no longer a residence but a tourist site. Sometimes, feeling the loss of what was, challenges me until I can become conscious of the possibilities resulting from the change.

Calling me was one of my former favorite cities, Sedona, Arizona. I say former because I have watched this city, full of spiritual sites honored by our ancestors, grow into a rather popular area. It just isn't the same for me anymore with buildings, golf courses, and even large grocery stores, everywhere. However, hiking out to Boynton Canyon and the Red Rock Crossing/Cathedral Rock area gave me the solitude and reflection I was looking for. Cogitating on the past three months at two of the swirling centers of energy in Sedona known as vortexes, was calming. It helped me see the sun between the clouds in an altered city. Just because these changes do not work for me does not mean they are unfavorable. What works for one person may not work for another. It is all good.

While exploring the great Southwest, I found myself assisting in a classroom on the Navajo Nation in Tuba City, Arizona, through an immersion program with Amizade, a Global Service-Learning nonprofit organization. This sweet experience rendered friends who welcome me for visits whenever I am in the area. While in Arizona, I found myself mesmerized by the Hopi mesas and the people who live in these villages. Residing for one hundred generations on the same land makes them one of the oldest cultures in North America. "Wow!" is all I can say. They are beautiful and welcoming people, just as I found the Navajo in Tuba City. My journey was opening my heart to all that is, without judgment or expectation.

Next on my itinerary was a visit to Chaco Canyon, which was a hub of ceremony for the Chacoan people from AD 850 to 1250. I was clear enough that I began to feel the energy of this sacred place in New Mexico. When I went to take pictures, I realized I had left my camera in my hotel room in Tuba City. My Navajo friend was so kind as to retrieve it and send it with her aunt who was going to be in Farmington that evening. The Universe had been listening again. As people continued to touch my heart through kind deeds, I learned how to feel outside the box where life is. This was my overhaul of what really matters and what brings me joy. Connecting with others allowed me to shift my perspective from victim to being inclusive of everyone.

Lest I forget to share all the head turners on my journey, I would like to mention other national and state parks and monuments that were sweet surrender to my time as I visited them. Sometimes I was so absorbed in the experience that I was forced out as the sun went down and the park closed. I recommend Walnut Canyon, Navajo National Monument, Monument Valley, Joshua Tree, and the Grand Canyon as some of our nation's treasures. Grounding into Mother Earth in all her glory is what I experienced while visiting these precious lands set aside for our enjoyment.

Bill Plotkin, author of *Soulcraft* and founder of Animas Valley Institute, writes about soul discovery and soul initiation. I was due in Durango, Colorado, the next weekend, where I spent an amazing three days with women who were on a journey to evoke a life-shifting experience based on Bill's work. My journey opened me to what was possible connecting with other women in ceremony and deep dialogue. Many years ago, I became certain that I did not learn the feminine aspect of life from my family of origin. I was getting a taste of what can exist between women who open to all that is. I was beginning to open myself to the possibility of having deep relationships full of trust, friendship, and love with other human beings.

While in the mountains, a storm ensued leaving the reservoir in Durango flooded and the distant mountains covered with snow. At the same time, in Tuba City, a tornado had touched down, which is a rarity. Clearly, Mother Nature was pushing me west. I did not like the thought of winter coming and altering my choices of travel. My acceptance of the flow of life right now, whether I liked it or not, was yet to come.

Slowly, I approached the state of California with the smog from fires, cars, and industrial pollution hanging in the air. The closer I got to the big city of Los Angeles, the heavier the smog became. It is said this smog moves east and hangs over the Grand Canyon. I was beginning to realize that my passion for travel was turning into my journey to wholeness. The exquisite Esalen Institute in Big Sur, California, was my next adventure and would play a crucial part in my recovery.

CHAPTER 6

Cleaning Bathrooms

(California)

"One does not become 'enlightened' only
by imagining figures of light and love,
but by making the 'darkness' conscious."
—CARL JUNG

While away from camp and traveling on my own, it became clearer and clearer how much I had gotten from Sufi camp: Strength and agility through exercising, detoxing with the vegan diet, losing a few pounds, breathing fresh air, and making many international friendships helped me peel layers off my "I'm okay, you're okay" façade. "Just leave me alone and everything will be okay." My wholeness wasn't as whole as I had imagined. The barriers were breaking down and my shadow was popping through the gaps. I was irritable, judgmental, and just plain not fun to be around. I was spiraling out into the dark night and not even aware that this was occurring. All my drumming, dancing, chanting, and hiking in nature was making my darkness conscious. I was beginning to question my limiting beliefs.

Sound heals our physical and emotional bodies. Along the way, we clear the negative frequencies weighing us down and keeping us from being our best selves. Feelings are not bad; they just are. All feelings, including negative feelings, go out into the Universe energetically. We are all connected through energy. I found myself in this state of intermittent negativity, pretending to be positive. I didn't intend to affect other people or myself, but I did.

So off I went to Esalen Institute in Big Sur, California, with a few doors to wholeness open and a lot of unpleasant feelings. Esalen has long been devoted to tapping unrealized human potential and fostering personal and social transformation, giving participants the opportunity to explore the deep recesses of their humanness.

I was beginning to panic. Somewhere at an unconscious level, I knew my life would be turned upside down on my path to wholeness. "We think too much and feel too little," said Charlie Chaplin, and being small was not part of my journey. In the next two months, the mood I was creating through my negative thoughts would present itself. I would be taken out of my head and into every imaginable feeling. I would become big as life along with my irritability.

It was all good. I was, after all, beginning to question my limiting beliefs. The panic in my body, mind, and heart seemed to be centered around concerns about "Who would I be if I didn't have these beliefs?" I wasn't sure I was ready to lose my identity, since I was very connected to who I had become and was sure it was the best way to be. I was compassionate (I thought), loving (I thought), nonjudgmental (I thought), and open to new ideas (I thought). But still there were the irritability and moods I didn't understand and most certainly didn't like.

My journey to Big Sur took me through Santa Monica to visit my friend Beverly. Together we went for an afternoon of contemplation at the Lake Shrine Temple and Retreat in Pacific Palisades. I found this center of meditation truly exquisite and peaceful. Especially impactful was the Court of Religions with the world's five main religions represented: Judaism, Christianity, Buddhism, Islam, and Hinduism.

This Court of Religions was inspired by Paramahansa Yogananda, who said, "There must be world brotherhood if we are to be able to practice the true art of living." The unity of all religions in one sanctuary encapsulates what Paramahansa and I know is true. We are all saying the same thing, just with different words. We are all connected. We are all one.

The delicious drive up Highway 1 kissing the Pacific Ocean most of the way led me to Esalen and my next adventure. My fears would be reckoned with on this brilliant, sunny, Sunday afternoon. I was assigned a bunk in a room with three other women. I had asked to work in the kitchen or in the garden, but was given cabin detail instead. Cabins meant I would be cleaning guest rooms, folding laundry, and— *scrubbing bathrooms.* For three days I pouted. Then I made an appointment with the coordinator to get reassigned, but to no avail.

It took a whole month to learn a new lesson, one of humility and acceptance. Finally, I gave up my old story, "I didn't retire from thirty years of teaching to clean bathrooms," for a new story, "Thank you for what you do to make this restroom clean for all those who use it." This is now what I say when I encounter the cleaning staff in a public setting. I am not better than another human being. We all want to be treated with love and respect.

At Esalen, all meals were eaten in the lodge overlooking the Pacific Ocean. Everyone dined together, even the cabin department and guests. Much of the food was organic, grown on the property, and prepared fresh in the huge kitchen. What a treat this was after eating on the road for six weeks, followed by vegan meals at Sufi camp. I was in my glory.

Evening relationship sessions were part of the Esalen Work Scholar Program. This group convened every day for the entire month. Getting to know others on property at a deeper level was a challenge. I am not sure if I succeeded completely, but I now have Esalen friends from all over the world.

My work group, the evening program, and one-on-one relating with other members of the community called for continuous processing. "Check-ins," as they were called, became part of everyday life. I was to share how I was feeling, what I was bringing to the encounter, how I was going to "show up," my appreciations, whatever was up for me at the moment. No one was going to let me hide on this property. Facing my core issues felt like mining with my arms wide open.

"Gestalting" they called it. I learned, "The whole is greater than the sum of its parts." "I" statements were reinforced, along with openness to change and grow. Experiencing the full range of emotions with honesty, and acceptance of myself and others were truly part of this Human Potential Movement. I embraced phrases such as:

- "I heard you say _____, and it felt _____."
- "When you said _____, what came up for me was _____."
- "How is this landing with you?"
- "I am having this reaction to the group: _____."

I gained the courage to share with other human beings how they impacted me. I grew in my openness to hearing how I impacted others. Giving up my defensiveness and becoming willing to talk in concrete terms rather than abstract phrases was huge for me. My entire being was breaking open and being exposed.

I returned to Esalen for a total of six months in the coming year. My position in the office during one of the months classified me as staff, allowing me to participate in workshops like Gabriel Roth's 5 Rhythms, which encouraged a spirit of aliveness in my body. I met inspiring people such as Robert Reich, author and secretary of labor under President Bill Clinton.

At an Esalen fundraiser, I won a Breema massage in a silent auction. A Breema massage assumes the body is just as it is meant to be, with nothing to be fixed. In other words, the body will heal itself and find balance through the support of the Breema practitioner in partnership with the recipient. The result is an incredible state of relaxation and well-being. By this time, I had acquired a focus on healing my body and heart so I could be in action with peak awareness. The Breema massage was aligned with my new focus.

After my first two months at Esalen, I headed north to Berkeley then Portland, Oregon, where my daughter, Melissa, lives. My trip took me through the beautiful Sierra Nevada mountains into the Cascade Range of northern California and Oregon. I love Mother Earth in all her majesty. Driving on Interstate 5 through mountain passes and cresting the summit only to have before me a majesty of mountain views was breathtaking. Thomas Kincaid had painted these views in glowing images many times. This moment gave me an inkling that I might be replacing my old story of victim with my new story of giftedness. But how could that be possible? I was only beginning to recognize my past injuries and understand them. Portland, my daughter, and Christmas 2006, here I come. I was ready to step away from the intensity for a while.

I had been traveling for six months and was raw from delving into the unknown and opening my heart to another way to be. Why did I deserve to be loved? The inspirational speaker Denis Waitley says it so eloquently, "It's not what you are that holds you back. It's what you think you're not." Even after living in community and processing daily in groups, I did not feel lovable. I was living behind a veil, not wanting people to know me. I carried an unconscious energy about keeping people at a safe distance and was continuing to push them away, as I had done my entire life.

I knew that only I could change the way I felt inside. The thoughts, beliefs, and feelings I was creating through negative patterns were manifesting in the physical world. "No one can make you feel inferior without your consent," Eleanor Roosevelt said. Would I ever shake this personal crisis, and if I did shake it, could it actually be my rebirth?

The visit with my daughter was delightful at the start. We attended The Nutcracker, a ballet Melissa and I had seen so many times during the holiday season. We broke bread together with plenty of mother-and-daughter time. Then her concerns about my lifestyle began to emerge. "Mom, no one else's mother does what you're doing. You don't even have a place to live. You're living out of your car." Her embarrassment was intense, and all I could do was reassure her that I was giving up a little to get a lot. I was on a journey and merely storing my things in my car.

What I didn't say was that I didn't know what I was getting from my journey at this point. I was still pretending this new life was fun and exciting. What I was not acknowledging was that my life was missing something, perhaps many things. I was bouncing around with my emotions—sometimes happy, sometimes sad, sometimes blissful, sometimes apathetic, sometimes feeling connected, other times disconnected. I left my daughter's condo and took a room in a hotel where I could immerse myself in a salt bath adorned with candles and soft music to ponder the meaning of life, and to cry.

I met Melissa for dinner the next evening and we connected heart to heart. Realizing that her mother was not living in her car but out of her car, that she was not living off other people but paying her way, made more sense to her. I explained that the exquisite experiences her mother was having created a space for growth and for a new person to emerge. This also helped ease my daughter's concerns. Our conversation would be the start of a daughter's supporting her mother on her journey to wholeness.

After a visit to the Cleveland area, where I usually stayed at Angel House in Strongsville, and reconnected with family, friends, and my aunt, I found myself in Boulder again, where my son, Tom, lived. We shared stories and reconnected. Tom was a huge support for me on my journey, as well. I didn't expect my children to take care of me. We were building mutual respect toward each other's choices and the deeper love that a healthy family embodies. I booked a room with a private bath in the Boulder region to breathe.

I found myself in the throes of processing all that had occurred for me in the last six months. My sweet space with Karen and her beautiful daughter, in Boulder gave me time to sit with my feelings and thoughts.

I browsed through my journals and notes from the first two months at Esalen, where I had found it difficult to stay connected with friends and family. I spent hours emailing them. The remoteness of Big Sur had been a good thing since it allowed me the space to go deeply into all that was stopping me from being the person I was born to be. The eventual reconnection with my former life was an essential part of fully processing my journey.

Was it the processing of all my emotions? Was it a physical issue? Whatever the cause, fatigue overwhelmed me the entire time I was in Colorado. Prior to leaving Cleveland, I visited numerous doctors and specialists to determine why I was not feeling well. The diagnosis of hypothyroidism and sleep apnea resulted in a need to take thyroid medicine and use a CPAP machine in order for me to sleep soundly each night. While traveling, I chose to use a sleep apnea dental device, which provided a lot of freedom over the CPAP machine. These remedies resolved just some of the "not feeling well" until an angel appeared in my life.

Dr. Sherri Tenpenny, DO, founder of Tenpenny Integrative Medical Center in Strongsville, Ohio, suggested an intracellular blood test rather than the traditional plasma blood test and found that I was extremely deficient in vitamin B12. She prescribed B12 syringes specially formulated without mercury that required refrigeration. I needed to inject B12 once a week and had to find a way to make it work as I traveled.

I watched my cold pack like it was breast milk for a baby. Each night I asked a hotel employee to place the syringes in the refrigerator and the freezer pack in the freezer. Though this was a minor annoyance at times, at the end of a year, my posttest proved that my diligence had not been in vain. My B12 levels were now in the normal range. My sense of confusion, memory loss, irritability, and lack of concentration had disappeared. The weekly self-injections and corrective devices for the sleep apnea had made a difference. I no longer felt as though I was moving into the state of dementia or Alzheimer's that my mother had been challenged with in her final years. But why was I still fatigued?

I became a fanatic about water. My 10 stage water filter was packed in a box in my storage unit and I missed it immensely. If I couldn't locate a Whole Foods to buy spring water and was uncomfortable with the hotel water, out came my SteriPEN. This device eliminates over 99.9% of viruses, bacteria, and protozoa that cause waterborne illness. I wasn't going to add any more illnesses to my potpourri of physical challenges.

PART III

Awakening

(pictured on previous page) The pathway at Esalen Institute that I walked up several times a day while living in the farmhouse and completing an internship in the Gazebo School Park. This pathway is my walk of transformation. I was truly challenged at Esalen to examine who I was as a human being...physically, mentally, emotionally and spiritually.

CHAPTER 7

Unexamined Assumptions

(Uganda)

When told the reason for daylight
savings time, the old Indian said,
"Only the government would believe
that you could cut a foot off the top of a
blanket, sew it to the bottom, and have
a longer blanket."

When I began my journey, my car had 80,000 miles on it. Arriving at Esalen four months later put me at the 90,000-mile mark. At the end of my journey, Old Betsy had 128,000 miles and had spent a total of 89 weeks, or 22 of the 48 months, sitting in the mountains of Boulder and Big Sur, or in condominium parking lots of friends around the western United States while I traveled oversees. About 12,500 miles per year is regarded as average. Considering the time my car sat in storage, I would place my mileage more realistically at 20,000 miles per year. As much as I enjoyed driving, there were many times I felt tired and longed to be rooted in one place.

On my final day in Cleveland in 2006, my sweet brother, Joe, helped me with the final tasks of moving out of my house of sixteen years. When he saw the pile of "stuff" in my living room, he told me I would never fit it in my car. I politely informed him that was my chore and would he please help me move everything from the garage to the donation center. After I'd loaded up the car, Joe shook his head, amazed that the view through the rear window wasn't even blocked.

What did I choose to take on my journey? My 2000 Honda Accord V6 provided ample space plus nooks and crannies in the front compartment that allowed me to store a lot of items: a backpack with my computer, camera, extra batteries and charger, sleep apnea dental device, passport, jewelry and herbal supplements. In the back seat, I had a pillow, sleeping bag and liner, two big and one small suitcase of clothes, a cooler, a bag of towels, AAA maps and travel books, two pairs of tennis shoes, hiking boots, thongs, sandals, a pair of nice shoes, a winter coat, a water bottle and vinegar to sanitize it with, a jug of fresh water, two types of natural bug repellent, sunscreen, a bag of toiletries, shampoo, and altar items.

In the trunk, I packed a sewing machine, two boxes of books, and a box of files that held information on the location of Honda dealers, the phone numbers of all my contacts (this is before smart phones were readily available), and my medical history, doctors, etc. I also had a toolbox, a box of assorted teas, first aid kit, a snow brush, a folding chair, a yoga mat, a bottle of windshield washer fluid, a CD cassette player, an iron, a fan and heater, photos, a box of kitchen items (can opener, knives, silverware, frying pan, pot and lid, toaster oven, thermos, hot water pot), food, and miscellaneous paraphernalia. I surprised myself with the thoroughness of my preparations for the journey amidst the sale of my house and a move to the storage unit.

Back in Boulder, I was attempting to regain my strength. The doctors were baffled. I tried Lugol's Iodine, which had worked for me in the past, and a potpourri of other items for ridding the body of fatigue. The reality was, some days I felt okay and other days not so well. The one thing I was not putting effort into was exercise. I used excuses: "I'm tired" or "The snow's too deep." Some days I became engrossed in the modern-day black hole—the computer, as I searched out my next venue. Travel was becoming an obsession for me. I suspect it was my way of running from the feelings that were quickly rising to the surface.

My next adventure came through a phone call from Amizade. I had spent a week on the Navajo Nation in Tuba City, Arizona, tutoring elementary school children following Sufi camp. I was being asked to return to Tuba City to help coordinate their Alternative Spring Break program for college students. I would assist in teaching about the Navajo life and culture. These students chose to make a difference during a week when many college students take vacations at the beach. I was truly excited about working with this organization and Sina, the teacher I had helped many months before. She is dedicated to maximizing her students' progress educationally, socially, and emotionally, and I so admired her. Sina and I would reconnect on behalf of our nation's youth to let them know we care about their education. As Hillary Rodham Clinton says in her book, *It Takes a Village.*

This month of co-facilitation with Amizade included three of the four weeks of March. Since I was not on duty one of the middle weeks, I drove to Las Vegas to sit at a pool in the warm sun and attend a Celine Dion show at the Bellagio. I had always wanted to experience Celine in concert and this was my chance. The experience lived up to my expectations. Her powerful and skilled vocals were more than music to my ears. They pierced my heart to the core in a way I will never forget.

Following my month on the Navajo Nation, I returned to Boulder and stayed with my son, Tom, for a few more days of reconnection. I also spent time with my community of choice, Dances of Universal Peace. Boulder became my home away from the home I had known for fifty-four years. The Universal Peace Dances, frequently led by Timothy Dobson, took me to places within myself to honor all traditions of the world. Timothy provided a space of quintessential spiritual practice in motion with eye contact, movement, and connective integration. I allowed the experience to reside within my being, feeling connected with everyone on Earth.

Hugs at the end of an evening of dancing provided more human contact and acknowledgment of who I am as a fellow human being. My soul was craving this piece of the human experience. Discovering a family of friends and exploring with like-minded individuals created a bridge for me as I journeyed deeper into who I was in relation to my past. I found everyone was a like-minded person if I chose to discover which like-minded piece was within our souls.

Spiritkeepers provided another opportunity to participate in the Dances of Universal Peace on a Sunday morning in Boulder. Sandwiched between the dances was a program presented by the community. It was through one of these presentations that I met Jo Noble. Jo is the founder and managing director of Partnering for Africa's Future, a nonprofit dedicated to sustainably empowering indigenous adults to build and grow independent businesses. She is also part of a management team working with eight-to-thirty-six-year-old professional musicians and dancers in Africa. Jo presented a program relating to successes and challenges with her work in Uganda. My eyes and ears perked up and my physical being stepped into action when conversing with her after the program. When she said to me, "Come to Uganda," I knew at that moment I would.

This experience would be my first international excursion on my four-year journey. My mind and heart would be torn open as Jo introduced me to responsible goodness and "how the powerful interact with the powerless," as Jo says. It is not an easy thing to get involved in other people's lives. I would gain a deep understanding of a culture intertwined with a tradition and a history that was not my own. I would only begin to become conscious of the strife these beautiful human beings have endured. I wanted to embrace their journey within my soul.

Arriving in Kampala, Uganda, after dark was surreal. As we drove to the house that would be my home for the next five weeks, I had my first taste of a different way of life. The absence of street lights provided a clear—or not so clear—view of the tiny fires outside the little huts where families and neighbors cooked their evening meal after the heat of the day had dissipated. I had traveled extensively, but this was about as exciting as it gets.

On day two, Jo's driver, David, took me by taxi into the city of Kampala. The objective was to provide me with tools to be as independent as possible. My first ignorant transfer of my American culture was experiencing people as angry because they did not smile back at me. What I would come to realize through Jo's kindness was that in this African culture, smiling can be an invasion of another's space, that these Ugandan people were smiling inside.

I was also immersing myself in a culture with a history of colonization, human rights violations, and government corruption. Long has there been disruption, betrayal, and violence in their lives. Why would they trust anyone? Neighbors turned on neighbors, foreigners imposed culture and solutions without having knowledge or interest in what the people wanted, and the government continued to support rebel groups and criminalize homosexuality. Trust is challenging and life ever fleeting. From personal experience, I knew about the challenges that come with building trust. This experience was taking it to the limits.

My teaching background gave me the opportunity to immerse myself in various educational settings. Jo put me in touch with the Kampala Baby Home where I traveled weekly to play with the babies and share songs and nursery rhymes with the moms, as the workers were called. The moms cared for the babies, infants to five years of age. While other Ugandan institutions taught English around the age of eight, after the child's native language was deeply embedded, the baby home taught English at a very young age. Knowledge and grasp of the English language provided an advantage for the babies to be adopted into a good home.

One of my eye-opening immersions was with a school in the village of Kymalinga. Jo knew Mr. Katamba, a plantation owner who had begun a school in his village so the little ones could be educated. Prior to the Kymalinga school, the closest walkable school was 20 miles. Only the older children could and would make this trek to attend classes.

Mr. Katamba and his family greeted us like we were royalty. They had prepared a meal by harvesting their fields and slaughtering a few of the small number of precious animals they owned. I felt truly honored. To top it off, they served us in their living room with their very best dishes and Ugandan finery.

Following our feast, we took a tour of their newly expanded school, with a library that had no books. I remembered beginning my teaching career at Washington Irving Elementary in the inner city of Cleveland without books. Resourceful as I sometimes am, I rescued books from the attic. I quickly became aware that there wasn't an attic for these teachers. Good nutrition and healthcare were almost more challenging than teaching without books. These teachers were on their own.

When the tour was over, the administration, the teachers, Jo, Kevin, and myself met in meeting format where we discussed the structure of the school in regard to finances, books, teacher pay, parent responsibility, student passage of government tests, etc. Jo was all about sustainability. She quickly realized that not enough parents were paying for their children's education. Thus, teachers sometimes were not being paid, etc. I was aghast that teachers who had never had a methods or child development class in college were teaching here. In fact, most, if not all, of them had never been to college. All I could say was wow! I could never have taught without this skill base. No wonder there was a high turnover of teachers.

Thus, the Uganda Teacher Fund was born. The teachers would attend college education classes at a satellite of Kampala University. I would raise funds for two-to-four teachers to attend on their vacation breaks. This scholarship would provide teachers the same opportunity as those in the capital city of Kampala. The teachers in Kymalinga, with little education and low salaries, had a strong desire to contribute to the world and their families.

A contract was drawn up to require a teacher to return and present the information and lessons learned to their fellow teachers. Thus a ripple effect would occur and the students would benefit greatly. The teachers who really cared began working harder. This village school became known in the region for its excellence. Parents wanted their children to attend a school where they would be educated and have new opportunities in life. Through Jo's savvy business ethics, 90 percent of the parents began paying their children's tuition. Jo then created resources for books, deworming, food, and a dormitory for teachers who traveled from a distance. The school grew from 107 students in 2005 to 409 students in 2011.

As qualified teachers were paid, more teachers wanted to teach in Kymalinga. The head teacher, Edith, began teaching the teachers and setting parameters in the classroom. No babies were allowed. Some teachers complained this would preclude them from working at their jobs. Edith stood firm, creating an environment for solutions to emerge. More elders cared for their young family members. The babies that came to school were watched by the cook who prepared the noontime meal out in the yard for the students who could pay. Teachers gave all their attention to the students, knowing their own children were properly cared for. It was a win-win situation, particularly for the future generation.

A sweet side to the story pertains to the acquiring of books. The Hawk Children's Foundation provided books and readers for the literacy program. But the teachers had never had books in their lives and didn't know how to use them. Edith rescued the situation by training the teachers. The whole paradigm shifted to that of a little village school in Uganda truly being a place of learning.

Additional challenges arose with the Uganda Teacher Fund. While I was providing funds for college tuition through Uganda presentations in the States, the universities in Uganda were requiring students to contribute photocopy paper and other supplies, buy uniforms, and pay their own travel expenses. Furthermore, they needed to provide for their own children and elderly parents while they were gone. By contract, we were asking for receipts for the fees they had paid, but a receipt was a foreign concept to a Ugandan village. And, silly me, in Uganda there isn't a legal system set up to enforce a contract.

Mr. Katamba provided the money for transport, I provided the funds for their college tuition, Jo provided the know-how and physical presence in Uganda, and Edith provided emotional and educational support. The teachers navigated the complexity to make it work, thus showing other teachers possibility and hope. This new paradigm in these teachers' lives meant they could not return to the old paradigm. A shift had occurred. They were on the road to incredible changes for themselves, their students, their families, and the entire village.

We did not come into Uganda as rich Americans with ideas to fix their challenges and tell them how to do it. A team systemically formed to support women in education to *step up* and *step out* as leaders in their community. I learned huge lessons on how the "powerful" can interact with the "powerless" and all can become more powerful. All people can help themselves and grow immensely in community. It is not an easy thing to get involved in other people's lives. As Nicholas D. Kristof and Sheryl WuDunn say in their book *Half the Sky*, "Women are indeed a linchpin of the region's developmental strategy."

Below is an excerpt from an email I sent to friends and family to update them of events on my journey.

My regret around the Uganda Teacher Fund is that I did not continue to support and raise funds for its continuation or expansion to other schools. I was too busy traveling, exploring, clearing past history, and finding my purpose in life. And the program did continue without me. Once a light is shone something, it grows. It was now in their lives and fellow teachers showed others that they could overcome complexity and make a passion work. They were confirming that people in community can help themselves.

Again, it is not easy to get involved in other people's lives. For instance, I had made lunch arrangements with a staff member at a Ugandan nonprofit for a brainstorming session. When she stood me up after I had paid the driver to take me to the restaurant, I became upset. What I didn't realize at the time was that the cost of lunch would have been equal to her weekly pay—and she still had to pay her transport since very few people in Uganda have cars. Just because workers in the United States may get paid lunch hours, doesn't mean people in developing countries do. Her time away would have cost her more money than I knew. I was awakening to how others experienced their lives.

CHAPTER 8

Daddy Longlegs

(New Mexico)

*"It is better that trials come to you in
the beginning and you find peace
afterward than that they come to you
at the end."*
—UGANDAN PROVERB

My return to the States took me to Cleveland where I presented programs on Uganda and explained the Uganda Teacher Fund. I found people were very curious about African traditions and way of life. My audience would soften into our cultural similarities rather than our differences. Women particularly could identify with other women across culture, race, and belief. They wanted to share with these incredible people, knowing we are all connected. The Ugandans had no idea how much they had given us in return. I was merely a conduit who came to Earth to love.

As I connected with other women around the world, my facade dropped more and more. I saw that others were not pretending, but I was. What was clearly playing out in my life was my lack of loving myself. Pretending I was happy and that I came from a happy and healthy family was just not possible anymore. I had to examine the behaviors of my family and former generations. The doors to family secrets were bursting open.

My reaching out to others in need was keeping me from examining my emotions. I always tried to "figure it out" rather than listen to my heart. I had figured out how to share my Uganda experiences and help others but I was not helping myself. The Ugandan teachers had shown me that once a light is shone on a situation, it grows. These women were growing and helping themselves, and now a bright light was beginning to shine on me. I was not willing to accept the pattern of denial any longer.

All disease begins with a thought, but feelings are the door to the soul. The guilt and shame were bubbling up like yeast in sugar water. I was so confused and distraught that I found myself in sessions with Jaclyn attempting to sort it out. Jaclyn helped me deeply experience the emotions and identify them. Somehow, they never felt like the bubbling yeast after a visit with her but more like a gentle flower opening for me to experience. By talking about my emotions, drumming, journaling about my memories while identifying how I felt, and spending time in nature, my pain eased. It was like peeling an onion layer by layer. I wasn't aware that I was peeling just below the skin of the onion and many more layers needed peeling before the bulb would be exposed. I was a fifty-four-year-young woman wanting to remove scar tissue from old wounds and was barely aware of this phenomenon.

Most of my adult life, I experienced allergy symptoms. My emotional congestion and my denial of who I truly was brought on the sneezing, runny nose, and physical congestion. As a survivor on a continuing journey, I did not acknowledge my worthiness of being healthy. It felt so unnatural to experience health and yet I was beginning to get glimpses of this condition. It would be two-and-a-half years before my living a healthy life became a way of being.

As I was leaving Cleveland on a plane, the pilot did something I had never experienced before and have not experienced since. On takeoff, he made a complete circle of downtown Cleveland and the Terminal Tower. From my window seat, I reviewed my life as I flew over my childhood neighborhood and the neighborhood in which I had raised my children. He then flew west along Lake Erie. I found myself crying and knew I would never live here again. It is because of my Cleveland experiences that I am who I am, and this city is near and dear to my heart. My friend, metaphysical teacher Ted Andrews, said, "We put to sleep one aspect of our life so another aspect can be awakened." I was putting Cleveland to sleep.

One week in Boulder was enough time to connect with my son, Tom, my many new friends, and my energy spots such as Artist's Point at the top of Flagstaff Mountain overlooking the valley. I found a rock in the middle of Boulder Creek to sit on and journal about the feelings I could identify. Identification was an ongoing process, thanks to Jaclyn's reminders. My visit with her prior to leaving Colorado left me with more tools to navigate my journey. I was truly in quantum theory mode with an energy that can heal the body and balance the emotions. I was experiencing the deep knowing that we are all the same no matter where we are in the world. We are connected with all life on this planet.

Longing for a space to call my own, I felt anxious to return to Sufi camp in New Mexico. Sufi camp would provide me with a tiny cubicle in a dormitory where I could keep my toiletries, snacks, hiking and exercise clothes, and water. During cold and stormy weather, I slept in my cubicle on a skinny mattress placed on the floor. I did not mind at all for this was my little corner of the world.

When the weather was pleasant and dry, I slept in a tent that I pitched in the forested area of camp. My favorite time of day was returning to my tent in the evening and falling asleep to coyotes howling, rain spattering on my tent, and other night sounds. Of course, having a toasty sleeping bag and a blow-up mattress helped to make the experience a comfy one. Upon waking in the morning, the sun would be shining through the sides of my tent warming everything for my emergence from my cocoon. I would lie quietly or doze and dream. My friends, the daddy longlegs, would always be standing guard over me. They were there in the morning peering down at me from between the tent screen and the rain flap, only to disappear for the remainder of the twenty-four-hour day.

The late Ted Andrews said that when daddy longlegs appear in our life, it "indicates increased awareness of what is going on around us, with greater ability to move in response to our perceptions." I was truly becoming more tuned in to all things in life. I was more aware of how I felt, what reaction I was having on others, and how to be different in the world. I was no longer insulated by family and friends, who would support me and seemingly understand everything that I said. I was my own person.

Out in this new world, the people in my life would call me on my choice of words, especially with my judgmental or sarcastic statements. I wasn't getting away with anything in my communications. I found myself baffled. It seemed I couldn't open my mouth without someone saying something to me. My response was one of anxiety. I was so in my story and blind to my limiting beliefs.

I scheduled myself to stay at Sufi camp for the next two months. It was a good way to clear toxins and get healthy by eating vegan foods, hiking, exercising, meditating, chanting, dancing, drumming, and just being removed from the constant hubbub of life in the United States.

People from all over the world would come and go, stay and leave Sufi camp. At the peak of the summer, there would be seventy-plus participants. It was exciting and challenging. While working and living with so many personalities, we would clear toxins from the body, as Adnan Sarhan guided us through the work, which required focus, patience, and compassion. Clearing noxious substances from the body at times created irritability, and yet the physical result felt so good.

As I freed myself from the physical constraints and found a freshness in my body, I also found staleness. I was experiencing negative feelings, memories, and hard-core beliefs coming to the surface. When easily irritated, I found myself missing my home in Ohio and regretting my decision to sell the house and most of its contents. My anxiety took me into ruminations about what I had and hadn't sold and what was in my storage unit. Was I merely diverting my feelings from my past abuse by creating anxiety about past objects? I wasn't ready to feel deeply all that is.

As emotions rose to the surface, I attempted to push them back down where they had been the better part of my life. I became more cantankerous to be around. I wanted to be left alone. If someone annoyed me, I would write them off as an unnecessary person in my life. If someone turned their back on me when I was reaching out to them, I would lunge like a rattlesnake, spitting out curt comments at the moment or at a later time. I would discount a person as valuable, then become baffled as to why they ended a conversation abruptly or didn't even acknowledge me. All the while, my feelings continued to froth to the surface.

The result was that I felt flawed. Something was wrong with me. All my life, I would blame myself when things didn't go the way I wanted. I would unknowingly push people away with my words and body language. Then I'd be confused, full of jumbled emotions, not knowing what was occurring. Even my thoughts would chime in. The feelings, thoughts, ruminations became so strong that I could not push them down anymore. So, I ran.

A Spanish visitor at Sufi camp, Char, and I were connecting on a similar energy level. We both wanted to leave. We hightailed it across New Mexico and into Arizona in my car under the ruse that camp was too confining. Tuba City was a definite stop on our journey. Unfortunately, I was not able to get in touch with my Navajo friend, Sina so we continued north on Route 89.

We stopped in Page, Arizona, to descend the exquisite Antelope Canyons with a Navajo guide. The Navajos have experienced the canyon as a spiritual place that uplifts them and puts them in harmony with something greater than themselves. Totally awestruck by the colors, wavy grooves, and beauty of this ancient site, I found myself communing with this celestial being we call Mother Earth. Knowing it was a rare moment in time, I did not want to leave and separate from this experience.

The following day we visited Glen Dam and its artificial reservoir, Lake Powell. This duo provides a huge water storage area and cheap hydroelectricity yet remains controversial with the alteration of the ecosystem in the Colorado River Basin. In the name of social justice, several man-made wonders of the world are being removed. This is another example of what power and wealth have done to the disenfranchised. Dams are built all over the world to divert water and create a source of electricity for big companies in big cities, leaving little or no water for people who have lived on the land with the river water for generations. An unexamined assumption that one person can take from another in order to have it all for themselves is creating the Occupy movements around the world.

When Glen Dam was built, territories like Southern Colorado and Mexico were ignored and are now drying up. Rethinking past decisions is crucial. Having the courage to do all we can to change what has been accepted as common practice is what will create a sustainable future for our great-great-grandchildren. Through my travels, I was able to see firsthand "engineering wonders" such as Glen Dam and begin to question my way of thinking, believing, and knowing.

Of course, I shared with Char two of our national treasures: the Grand Canyon and Sedona, Arizona. I find myself mesmerized whenever I see the depth and breadth of one of the Seven Natural Wonders of the World, the Grand Canyon. It leaves me awestruck every time. We stopped at Sedona for the allure of the energy vortexes, the spirituality, and the red rock scenery. Many times over the last decade, this city has left me feeling nourished and enriched. Unfortunately, it continues to be encroached upon by man, thus it is harder to experience the power of this once-special mecca for seekers. The continual building of resorts, golf courses, and housing developments is fast and strong, yet you can still feel much of the area's energy and power. I particularly love Boynton Canyon and the Cathedral Rock area. Char appreciated the experiences over our five days together.

After our getaway, I stayed at Sufi camp for an additional week, taking time to clear out the toxins from our trip. As I got healthier and healthier, I realized how difficult it was to find food free of herbicides, pesticides, genetic modification (GMOs), partially and fully hydrogenated fats, high fructose corn syrup, and the myriad of other cancer-feeding sugars. I was especially aware of my challenge to eat nourishing foods when I traveled. Often I would Google "Whole Foods" and stock up my cooler with organic foods to eat for the next few days. I highly recommend reading labels and knowing the source of the food you eat. It is quite amazing that we ship food back and forth across continents and oceans and buy this shipped food in stores, even though we have incredible food grown or produced in our own neighborhoods. I would rather save the petroleum used in shipping for a later date when I want to fly to visit one of my children. I haven't figured out how to stockpile oil but the big oil companies sure have.

A picture of my home in Cleveland, OH which sold in three weeks as the market began to plummet and the average home took ten months or longer to sell. I do believe the Universe was giving me the message to begin my journey sooner rather than later.

My cubby home at Sufi Camp was a nice respite on stormy nights rather than retreating to my tent in the forest which sometimes became drenched. I didn't mind not having all the luxuries of my old home but I did miss my own bathroom.

I had the pleasure to hike one evening on the Navajo Nation in Arizona where we climbed up to the top of a mesa. The expansive view over the land was heavenly and I felt honored to be invited on this very special land.

Seeing the big picture in regards to cleaning bathrooms and working in laundries finally puts a smile on my face. I so appreciate all human beings making a living by working in hotels and public washrooms cleaning up after others.

Women drying children's clothing and bedding on the ground in the warm sun at a hospital in Kampala where we did Dances of Universal Peace with HIV-positive young adults.

Mount Agung is spiritually significant to the Balinese. It is home to the Mother Temple of Besakih and overlooks the fields where we took a rice paddy hike.

After a long day of massage classes and writing curriculum, I sometimes explored the jewels of the Balinese culture with my classmates from around the world. This is me with a clown after a Kecak Fire Dance in Uluwatu Bali.

Men performing the Kecak Dance at the BaliSpirit Festival with their hands raised to the sky. Sharing culture is a joy of mine and these men invited guests to join them in the ceremony. Of course, I said yes.

My love of Brazil included my love of the old and the new. This picture was taken in the small town of Alto Paraiso depicting the Brazilian environmental consciousness with recycling bins amidst the public telephone. There are cities around the world where recycling is unheard of even today.

A sunrise excursion to view dolphins on a typical Balinese fishing boat in the Bali Sea just off the North Shore of the island. We floated over coral reefs which were brilliantly viewed through the crystal clear water.

Iguazu Falls is located on the border of Brazil and Argentina and currently has the greatest average annual water flow of any waterfall in the world. The falls is on the UNESCO World Heritage List.

Favela's or shanty towns in Brazil are neighborhoods for the poor who were initially pushed out of the cities and later came from rural areas. Shanty towns being impoverished areas are inhabited by drug lords and generally off limits for tourists. I took this picture of a Rocinha Favela passageway on one of the few tours available in Rio de Janeiro.

With Pachamama Alliance guides, we slept in tents in the Ecuadorian Amazon outside this Achuar home. The Achuar live simply and sustainably always giving back to Mother Earth thus embodying an interconnectedness with all life. In partnership with the Pachamama Alliance, the Achuar are inspiring a new dream of a just and sustainable human presence on this planet.

My childhood home in Cleveland which was boarded up upon my return to the states. I don't believe the boarded up house was an accident and within months, it was razed and the steps on the right (i.e.book cover) were removed as well. The Universe was conspiring with me to release all childhood abuse issues which were stopping me from being a person who shares her gifts and makes a difference for all life on the planet.

CHAPTER 9

On Being a Tree

(California)

*"It is better that trials come to you in
the beginning and you find peace
afterward than that they come to you
at the end."*
—UGANDAN PROVERB

Visiting my daughter after Sufi camp was a delight. Melissa always greeted me inside the airport with Cassie, a young girl she mentors through the Big Brothers Big Sisters program. Cassie kept a rescue rat from Oregon, called Julian, in her pocket. When we entered Melissa's tiny downtown Portland apartment, we were all greeted by Toby and Casey, two little dogs Melissa had adopted from rescue agencies in the Midwest, and Bella and Rosealie, ferrets rescued in Oregon along with Julian. We were one big happy family.

Melissa, Cassie, Toby, Casey, Bella, and I would pile into Melissa's Honda Civic with a cooler of drinks and sandwiches for lunch. As usual, Rosealie stayed home and Julian was in Cassie's pocket. A day at Cannon Beach on the Oregon coast allowed us to connect with each other and with Mother Earth on a cellular level. Soaking up the magnificence of the ocean with a few of the most important beings in my life created a grounding into what was most important to me. It was sheer bliss.

The close proximity of Portland and Seattle and the myriad of cruise ships setting sail for Alaska gave me the opportunity to experience a direction in my journey. I sent an email out to friends and family inviting anyone to join me on a last-minute deal on an Alaska cruise. Delightfully, my former sister-in-law, Angela, jumped at the opportunity. Angie is like a sister to me. The opportunity to visit our northernmost state and share it with a person I felt special affection for was music to my soul.

Mother Nature in all her glory graced us with one of the best Alaska weather weeks of the season. It didn't rain until the last day, when we were in the Inside Passage. We had already seen Juneau, Skagway, Tracy Arm Fjord, and Prince Rupert. Even in the rain, the beauty of the Inside Passage kept me on the ship's deck long enough to wreck havoc on my camera. All in all, the experience was as delightful as the person I was experiencing it with.

The next several weeks were spent in Boulder assisting Jo with a Uganda presentation and in Cleveland presenting a Sufi workshop and Uganda presentation. Most of my life had been spent teaching in front of our nation's youth, although my comfort level in front of adult audiences was increasing along with my presentation skills. I was coming from a place of service rather than a place of need. The power in being unattached to the outcome and trusting myself was huge in presenting effectively to adults.

I was just beginning to see that others experienced me differently when I *stepped up* and *stepped out* with my own uniqueness. I was shedding the fear of what other people thought by sharing what inspired me. So, what did inspire me? People and nature. This was true wealth. I was just beginning to reap some of the benefits of the hard work I was doing in clearing my childhood issues. As I peeled the onion, life got easier.

My trustworthy car was in Boulder with my son. I flew to Colorado to retrieve it and continue on my journey. I had been accepted as an intern in the Gazebo School Park for children at Esalen Institute and I would once again return to live on Big Sur, this time for a total of four months—for some more onion peeling.

Hopi Mesa

Two weeks prior to the start of my internship, I began the drive from Boulder to Big Sur. I had more than 1,200 miles of driving ahead of me but this time I didn't mind. There were exciting encounters in store. My drive took me through favorite places, like Sedona, the Hopi Reservation, and Tuba City. Unfortunately, I did not arrive in Sedona as quickly as I had expected.

Old Besty, my 2000 Honda Accord, had almost 100,000 miles on her when I heard a clunk, clunk, clunk in the front end. I was leaving the Hopi Reservation after experiencing the Women's Society Dances. I drove slowly for many miles and eventually found a hotel on Route 66 as the sun was going down. It was Saturday night, when most mechanics were at home with their families. I parked Old Betsy and spent the night in a hotel room eating the remaining food in my cooler.

The following morning, I decided to make the drive to a larger city where repair shops could easily be found. I hadn't traveled far when the clunk got louder. I listened to my feelings about this predicament and decided my driving miles were numbered. I called my sweet brother, Joe, who got on his computer to find me a garage. After a time, Joe and I agreed I would need a tow, even if it was a Sunday afternoon in October. Finding myself in a remote area of Arizona, I was challenged to describe my location to the insurance company towing dispatcher. (Later, I would add the luxury of GPS to my cell phone.) With my brother's help, I was able to tell them my location and was towed to another hotel by the nearby repair garage. Another lonely day and night in a strange hotel.

The following morning, I used AAA to tow me to another garage. It took less than fifteen minutes for the mechanic to determine that the lug nuts had jiggled loose on one of the wheels. Happily for me, what could have turned into a disaster ended up a simple fix. Off I went to Sedona and Tuba City to visit friends.

A walk through Sedona's Boynton Canyon helped me to settle my emotions and regain the excitement about the coming months. This time in Tuba City, I was fortunate to spend time with my friend Sina and to visit the beautiful new school completed for the education of our nation's youth. The children were being honored, deservedly so, with a place of knowledge that rivals our nation's government buildings. Whoever said children deserve less than this? Saying good-bye to Sina was bittersweet. Thank goodness for Facebook.

My next stop was Los Angeles to join the *Dr. Phil* show audience. I had gotten tickets at a silent auction fundraiser for the Samburu Project. Supporting this nonprofit, which eases Kenyan women's daily struggle by providing wells for access to clean water, was an easy decision. The *Dr. Phil* show was filming a discussion with the family of Nicole Brown Simpson and O. J. Simpson's ghostwriter. My eyes were opened and my heart expanded for the victims of this tragedy.

Several months earlier, I was accepted as a volunteer with Syn-chroDestiny, a five-day program designed and facilitated by Deepak Chopra to assist people in recognizing the possibilities that unfold around them. Creating what we want in life by manifesting our dreams, wishes, and desires is possible. I had attended many programs facilitated by Dr. Chopra and used his primordial sound meditation daily. This incredible opportunity provided me with higher experiential learning in quantum physics and helped me segue into my Esalen participation. Creating what I want with effortless ease was what I was looking for. SynchroDestiny reinforced for me what I knew to be true about all of life. I was ready to put an end to the continuous hard life I was buying into.

Returning to Esalen as an intern in the Gazebo School Park meant I would have a room in the farmhouse, which sits on a cliff overlooking the Pacific Ocean. Each day for four months, I would open my bedroom door to peer at this wonder of nature. Three times a day, I strolled across the lush grounds to the lodge to eat my meals, which were prepared consciously for the nourishment of staff, workers, and participants. Wow! When I was raising my children as a single parent, working full-time as a teacher, and taking classes in the evening toward my master's degree, no one ever made meals for me or my family. What a treat this was. Often after eating, I could go to the baths overlooking the Pacific Ocean and soak till my heart's content, feeling like I was in heaven.

The Gazebo School Park functions as an ecologically based program serving children infancy to six years. These lucky children have the opportunity to immerse themselves each day in the natural world. As a group, we would be outside rain or shine for all activities including eating, art, dramatic play, etc. I believe, during the entire time I interned in the program, we were inside due to inclement weather just a half-dozen times.

The first month, I was instructed to spend my day as a "tree," observing the children and other teachers without getting into the energy space of the children. I then journaled my observations, feelings, and experiences. Having been formally trained in Western education and having served in the capacity of teacher at all grade levels for thirty years, I believed at the cellular level that I was an excellent teacher. I could provide evidence that children needed adults to teach them.

After raking leaves, edging, and weeding full-time for four weeks, my deep beliefs were still ingrained in me. The director of the school, Cath, managed to see through my facade and knew I was not ready to interact as a teacher. I was pronounced to another week as a "tree." Trees were to interact with the teachers and animals only—three goats, one pig, and many chickens. I was also permitted to clean up toys, organize learning areas, and prepare lunches. All in all, I was majorly distressed and felt like a teacher's helper.

Week six brought an easing into the role of teacher. Imagine, here I was with my Master of Education degree and I wasn't appropriate for interacting with young children. I remained baffled, cognizant that I had committed to four months as an intern. My path in life was to remain committed to integrity, so for a time I would be at peace with my decision, then I would become frustrated again. What was up for me at this point in my life was learning that I did not know everything. I would soon become open to learning more about children, education, and teaching. A hard lesson for me was the humility of it all. I just wasn't as important as I believed myself to be.

As I eased into my interactions with the children, I felt frustrated and awkward. I didn't know what to say, how to say it, or how to be in this new paradigm. I was no longer the person who must impart knowledge. I was beginning to see that children could learn through exploration and interaction with their peer group. They could actually teach me!

The beautiful, sunny days on Big Sur flew by as I began to decipher how to speak to our precious youth and where I could healthily intervene in their process. I could now clearly see when they were "in their process" or "in a state of observation and learning by doing." This state of being is invaluable for emotional and mental growth. Saying something and intervening stumps this growth process.

All the while, as an intern teacher, I was learning about my process and how to be in the moment. Teachers are great learners and we teach what we want to learn. However, what if we taught through our own state of being and observed others in their process? What if we didn't force others to learn what we want them to learn? What if teachers gave up the shoulds, coulds, and woulds, and just allowed others to be in their process in the present moment? Imagine if teachers didn't tell others how to do something "better." Suppose we didn't crush the self-esteem of our youth. Would our species' "genius" begin to pop through so that all of humanity could benefit?

As with all work groups at Esalen, the adults would process daily for twenty minutes before the students arrived. Processing is sharing with others how we are "being" so others know where we are coming from emotionally. Likewise, we would process in an adult group with the staff psychologist or a facilitator trained in somatic therapy. Somatic therapy integrates our mental, emotional, spiritual, and physical aspects by assisting us to become aware of our bodies and the sensations we experience. By paying attention to how the body is feeling, we can begin to make connections with our feelings and become more aware of what we are experiencing. Somatic therapy is great for all of us. It was particularly helpful to me, who had shut down all emotions to protect myself from abuse. This daily process began to help me get in touch with who I was becoming—an open, connected, and emotive human being.

In our two-hour sessions, we would discuss issues concerning the children and agree on an approach so we would all be on the same page. We could also bring up personal issues, if that's what was "up for us." One day I wanted to talk about a young boy who appeared to be a bully and did not interact with either children or adults in a fair manner. I was asked if he reminded me of anyone. Immediately, one of my brothers came to mind. The next question was, "How would my brother be dealt with by my parents?" What I said was, "My father would have smashed him alongside his head." This answer opened the door for me to attend a month-long evening Gestalt Therapy Group. And so a new journey began for me.

The Gestalt group focused on the awareness of my life in the present moment. It was also about a richer, deeper path to wellness, or personal clearing and emotional release. As my life was reflected and clarified, I waited to see what would unfold. After all, I had processed my past already and had cleared all the emotional baggage, or so I thought. I began to get curious about what more there might be for me to work through emotionally.

"Intense" is the first thing I will say about my evening program in Gestalt. To ease the tension, I increased the number of massages I was getting and attended as many early morning movement classes that I could drag myself out of bed for. I was descending into my body and emotions through all that was available. Esalen is known as a place to go deeper into the body, mind, spirit, and heart. The community was living up to its promise.

Everything about my childhood, growing up with multiple siblings, unfolded. The pain inflicted by an abusive father and my siblings who had learned so well from him was continuing to surface for examination. It was excruciating looking at the abandonment I felt from a mother who was a victim herself, deeply depressed and frozen in time. She had no idea how to create a different life for the children she birthed and loved immensely. I loved her and began to look at the anger I had toward her for not being in my life to protect me, as a mother ought to do.

This unfolding contrasted my very nature of being. My Catholic upbringing taught me to stuff the anger and resentment in order to be the good girl. I was the quiet one who, if I wasn't seen, would be less likely to be preyed upon. My childhood experiences so contrasted my teachings by the Church that denial closed me up in a locked vault with the key at the bottom of Lake Erie. I was beginning to swim deeply and would not find the key for months to come. It was all good, albeit painful. It felt like I was eating an artichoke heart from the inside out, all the while crying and feeling fury toward my perpetrators. If it was unpleasant to be around me before, it was really challenging now. I was raw, vulnerable, and grieving, feeling love for myself was not even possible as I swirled down the rabbit hole.

In the past, Jaclyn had assisted me with anger. Sometimes I would beat a drum for hours or journal ugly thoughts for those who had been perpetrators. Now with the intensity turned up, I was guided to utilize healthy ways to get at the anger without lashing out at other people, even those who had hurt me. I reached deeply into my soul to clear the abuse.

The Gestalt approach gave me a safe space to let anger out, and let it out I did—punching pillows and using words I had only heard before in my life. Now these words and gestures had an audience, creating a catharsis and powerful clearing for the pain. Releasing the anger opened portals to emotions that had been stuffed for much of my life. The portals closed somewhat with diversions, such as working with the children or driving from Big Sur to Monterey. Yet, they never closed completely, thank goodness. I was not yet finished with my work.

My time at Esalen, and especially my time in the Gazebo School Park, taught me many things I had closed my eyes to. One of the profound lessons was that children learn in spite of adults, not because of them. I also learned some basic ways to be, such as knowing that I am completely responsible for my thoughts, words, and actions. People can heal their wounds and grow in compassion, kindness, and love given the safety, support, and tools to do the work.

Additional lessons took the form of deep observation. I watched children learn about their bodies by scampering up trees, climbing on rooftops, and spending their days in nature rather than behind brick walls. We all were connecting with the source of life, and that was empowering and enriching for me. For the first time in my life, I milked a goat, fed a pig, and gathered eggs each morning with my new friends, the children infancy through six years of age. We made juice from fresh organic apples and oranges and ate all our meals outside. The energy of the children coupled with the energy of Mother Earth was sweet, healing, and grounding for me. What better way to be open and vulnerable to my past than in this delicious healing sanctuary, Esalen Institute?

PART IV

Deepening

(pictured on previous page) Monkeys at the temple in the Sacred Monkey Forest in Ubud, Bali. Notice the mother, father and two children. True Sweetness.

CHAPTER 10

Peeling the Inner Layers of the Onion

(Bali)

"Learn to get in touch with the silence within yourself, and know that everything in life has purpose. There are no mistakes, no coincidences, all events are blessings given to us to learn from."
—ELISABETH KUBLER-ROSS

The exploration of the human potential can best be explained by saying it is the incorporation of all facets of the human experience (physical, mental, emotional, spiritual) as the self, in community and the world through ecology, psychology, and sustainability, to name just a few modes. My name Carolyn means "courageous one" and my nature is adventurous. Esalen opened up opportunities to meet in person and speak to such thought leaders as Jean Houston and Michael Murphy.

I had the opportunity, as well, to build my core strength with Gabriel Roth, Kathy Smith, and Ellen Watson, among others.

Ellen Watson was a pioneer at the inception of Esalen. She continues to teach movement classes and give massages on the cliffs of the Pacific Ocean in the exquisite Esalen baths. She also teaches massage and dance in various countries around the world. I found myself drawn to her energy, style of teaching, and worldly experience. During one conversation she said to me, "Are you an academic? Do you write curriculum?" I had never thought of myself this way before. But now I realized I had written curriculum in my teaching career and had put in many hours of studying teaching methods and what works in education. I would go to Bali to write curriculum for Ellen.

It wasn't long before I had my travel visa and was on my way to one of the most delightful, spiritual islands in the world, Bali. I spent seven weeks doing yoga, exploring dance, learning massage, and writing curriculum. I expanded my horizons in each of these areas in the middle of the rice fields, flora, and fauna of Indonesia.

As I was being transported to the resort where I would spend six of the seven coming weeks, my first impression was that of a doubting Thomas. Everywhere I looked there were shrines of varying sizes with handmade gifts to the gods made from woven bamboo, flowers, rice, and crackers. From my limited perspective of the world, it felt like a tourist trap display luring people to view a staged way of life. But I soon learned these people were for real. The Balinese sincerely honor the gods with every step of their day. Their worship is heartfelt, sincere, and part of their every being. I immediately felt accepted by the Balinese people and appreciated for who I was. I deepened into my love for this culture and its people, not unlike my love for Ugandans.

My cottage room was open to the air with a view of waterways, rice fields, beautiful gardens, and swimming pools. At night, I would lower the bamboo shades and my mosquito net and fall asleep to the sounds of geckos on my ceiling. The night sounds lulled me into a beautiful deep sleep, and the birds outside gently awakened me to begin my day.

The Bali Spirit Fest was launching its first annual yoga, dance, and cultural festival during my first week in Bali. I wouldn't have missed the dancing, playing, and exercise for a minute. Of course, this conscious community of expats and islanders also provided healthy organic foods and drinks for the entire first week of my stay. I was immersed in a healthy lifestyle once again and felt like I was in heaven.

During the second week, I started my day with yoga, then a breakfast of organic food in the restaurant overseen by Ellen. Nurturing the body with healthy food was crucial in keeping up with Tami's yoga or with Ellen's masterful ways of instructing us in dance. Following breakfast, we would walk across walkways and bridges through the rice fields to the wantilan, where dancing was the theme of the day. For five days, Ellen led us in processes to build strength, coordination, and stamina through movement. My love for dance, particularly individual movement, helped me further peel the onion and release the outrage over my past. My previous month of Gestalt had set me up for dance as a healthy, cathartic outlet.

In the third week, Essential Touch Massage gave me the opportunity to learn a new skill. My delight in the program had much to do with Ellen's involving people from all over the world. Focus on the skills was essential for me, as Balinese and Japanese interpreters assisted non-English speakers in grasping the artistry and technique of massage. All the while I was learning the skills and partaking in the kinesthetic practice, I took notes in a step-by-step fashion on the how-to and the assessment of learning. I'd return to my room in the evening after dinner to write curriculum for several hours. After all, that is why I came to Bali. I would be assisting Ellen in exchange for my experience of dance, yoga, and massage. By the end of the month, I presented Ellen with more than a hundred pages of a course of study for this branch of knowledge.

Massage had always been one of my favorite techniques for relaxation and stress relief. When I worked as a high school teacher and department chairperson, I treated myself once a month to counteract the high stress of the job. Massage was invaluable in bringing me back to a relaxed state for Monday morning. Throughout my six-month stint in Big Sur, I treated myself to an Esalen massage on the cliff overlooking the Pacific Ocean. The experience was delicious, adding to my journey toward health.

Never did I desire to be a massage therapist or envision myself giving a massage. My experience with massage in Bali, however, quickly helped me realize the therapist is receiving similar benefits as the recipient. I was loving the whole process: learning anatomy and physiology, energetically connecting with the person I was massaging, and becoming well versed in the technique of massage. After learning a new skill, we practiced massage on each other. Typically, we did this twice daily with multiple practice sessions on the weekend.

By the third week, I was quite relaxed. I hadn't realized more layers of the onion had been peeling away. I was so busy learning, practicing, and writing that I was no longer in touch with what my body and emotions were experiencing. With that said, Vicki, one of the most popular massage therapists at Esalen, arrived in Bali to assist Ellen with the teaching. She offered to do a full massage for anyone wanting the full experience rather than individual technique massages. My body and emotions spoke to me and I jumped at the opportunity. After all, I had attempted to schedule a massage with Vicki while on Big Sur but our schedules never jibed.

That Saturday afternoon, my very being was looking forward to an exquisite massage in the wantilan in the middle of the Balinese rice fields. Part of our teaching was to communicate our needs and experience with the therapist. After about thirty minutes, my oohs and aahs transformed into a deeply emotional phenomenon. Vicki was aware that strong emotions were surfacing for me. After fifty minutes of expert massage, my tears came in torrents.

My month of Gestalt process, weeks of dancing and yoga, and two massages per day were breaking through the defenses I had spent a lifetime building. I bawled like a baby as the memories, emotions, and all that was in my past came pouring out. It was a breakthrough into my locked box. I had found the key. I no longer felt the stiffness of "Good girls don't tell family secrets" and "Abuse never happens to pious young Catholic girls."

I cried for weeks, literally. I cried for the last week of massage and cried while I wrote curriculum. I cried at Prana Dewi Retreat Center in northern Bali where I went for my final week overseas. I cried in the morning when I sailed out into the Bali Sea to dolphin-watch and I cried for weeks after returning to the United States. I had no idea there was so much bottled up inside me or that I could cry so much. When my eyes could cry no longer, my heart took over. My entire being shook and pulsated until there was nothing left for my heart to shed. The day had come when the risk to remain a completely formed onion was more painful than peeling the layers. I had reached the core. I could respond or not, and I responded in a big way.

It would be a long time before I felt balanced and like myself again. I questioned whether this deep pain was required in order to be strong and stand in my power. Deep down, I always knew I wanted to do something big with my life. Was this clearing really necessary for me to share my gifts? Little Anthony and the Imperials sing "It Hurts So Bad." I was resonating with this song, no longer looking for something outside myself.

The biggest culprits of depression are dehydration, sugar, and preservatives. As I continued my four-year journey, which would soon take me into Brazil, I monitored what I ate and where I ate my food. Jaclyn shared with me that Mother Nature could hold me in her care at times when I was feeling challenged. I could envision being encased in the arms of a fern, fluffed by clouds, or nourished by the feminine energy of water. I would take long, warm sea salt baths, light a candle, and play my favorite music. I would choose carefully what I exposed my skin to since skin absorptions go right into the blood. I was cleansing my body, mind, and heart all at once and would ask myself, "What is the most loving thing I can do for you today?" Most days, it was walking in nature.

Emotions give me a message. In its Latin form, the word "emotion" means to move forward. Now was the time for me to be courageous, to express through writing or words just what emotions were coming up for me, and to move forward. I wasn't feeling movement inside, only frozen in time. Through Jaclyn's guidance, I came to the intelligence of the heart, which is more powerful than the intelligence of the mind. More information goes from the heart to the head than from the head to the heart. I was now listening to my heart and would finally forgive at a deep soul level. At all cost, I was going to become the person I was meant to be.

I reached a point in my saga when I could begin to laugh again. I surrounded myself with high-vibration people and returned to Esalen, this time as a guest. I slowly began to appreciate my epiphany massage with Vicki and encountered the breakthrough of who I was becoming. I was pleased with the tranquility of my stay at Esalen and grateful for the reconnections with some very special friends. With this support in my life, and Jaclyn's, little by little, emotional fluency returned to my life.

"Ask for what you want and be prepared to get it," says Maya Angelou. I had always wanted to relieve myself of the gaping hole in my soul, the tapes playing in my mind, and the fear that my life would never make a difference. In working on the "Big Daddy"—anger, something began to shift. I was moving from the jammed unhealed wounds into a new way of thinking and feeling. I had come face to face with the truth and began a huge personal transformation of my old pattern of victimization. I was creating a satisfying life by gently pushing through what was scary. Still, it would be many months before I reached a yin and yang balance in my wild and crazy life.

Stepping out into my true essence did not come easily. With 70 to 80 percent of behaviors in the subconscious, it would be a while before I trusted the heart. There was a disconnect at the moment between who I knew myself to be and who I envisioned myself to be. I was now on a conscious journey to *step up* and *step out* to live a powerful life. I had no idea how I was impacting others or how I could live more fully. Jaclyn continually guided me to reconnect with my feelings. I held on to a puzzling deep connection with my immediate family and the dysfunctional patterns of behavior. The last remnants of hurt blocked me from freedom. I was still living in the past and fearing the future as though I was in a time warp. I wanted to surrender and accept, yet the blame, shame, guilt, and judgment kept me from optimism and hope for the future. I was in a time-space illusion and didn't know what I felt.

CHAPTER 11

There Is Energy in the Field

(Brazil)

"The time has come to turn your heart
into a temple of fire."
—JALALUDDIN RUMI

After visiting Esalen as a guest, I spent a week in a condominium in Lake Tahoe, California. My children flew in to join me for four days. As we absorbed nature through our daily hikes, we made a pleasant though bittersweet reconnection, since I knew I would not see them again for three months.

I spent the remainder of the week preparing for my nine-week journey to South America, which took me out of my feelings and back into my head. I would experience six weeks in Brazil and three weeks in Ecuador, with a week in Florida sandwiched in between. All major U.S. airlines fly north and south, so it seemed as though I would end up in Florida no matter what choice I made. I capitalized on the location to visit my sister and her family.

I had a lot of organization to do for two entirely different trips and needed to gather the necessary belongings from three different locations: my car, my storage unit in Ohio, and the local travel store. I wanted to ship my items for Ecuador to my sister's so I didn't become physically burdened with such things as a duffel bag, hiking clothes, and a travel book while in Brazil. When I returned from Brazil, I would pick up the Ecuador box in Florida and mail a box of Brazil items to a friend in Cleveland. This was a chore since I needed to sort through my car and donate unneeded items to the Goodwill. I was amazed at how much I had accumulated in my car. Sometimes, too tired to sort through the car, I had just piled the items in. Most people didn't realize I was virtually living out of my car. Fortunately, I never needed to sleep in it.

Photography was becoming more and more a passion of mine. Two years into my journey, I had thousands of photos downloaded on my computer. I had heard horror stories of computers crashing and people losing all their photos, so I spent two days in the Lake Tahoe condominium organizing my photos and backing them up to an external hard drive and CDs. Computer technology was not something I was fluent in, so it took hours trying to figure it out.

Staying connected with friends and family was very important to me. I typed lengthy emails telling of all the wonderful experiences I was having on my journey. Rarely would I mention the challenges, thus making traveling the world out of my suitcase and storage unit sound glamorous. I was free of mortgage payments, house repairs, the daily grind. At this point in the four years, I was truly disconnected from everyone, emotionally, physically, and on a reality level. A very dear friend from college once said to me, "It's nice that you are having a good time but not everyone in Cleveland is." I was insensitive to the picture I was painting and the impression it was giving. I was pretending to be sensitive but, in reality, I was insensitive and disconnected from my life in my hometown. I was in a zone of what Carolyn Rose Hart's life was like, and no one else's.

Following my visit to Cleveland, where I connected with the family and friends I had become disconnected from, I dealt with another logistical issue: My automobile license plates and e-check would expire while I was in Brazil. My car was registered in Ohio, was currently in California and Nevada, and would be in Arizona for three months during my Brazil trip. Plus, my e-check was due for renewal. Fortunately, with much discussion, I was able to obtain a one-time waiver from Ohio. I would somehow need to get the car e-checked in Nevada, sent to Ohio, and the new sticker to a friend in Arizona. I had to meet this friend prior to flying to Brazil with the Phoenix Friendship Force International Group and place my new license sticker on my car. Whew!

Friendship Force International is an exchange program initiated by President Jimmy Carter to foster goodwill among the peoples of participating countries. Since its inception in 1977, it has brought together millions of people from all over the world as unofficial ambassadors exchanging culture, ideas, and friendship through home hosting. I had served as vice president of the Northeast Ohio Chapter prior to selling my home. Now, traveling with the Phoenix Friendship Force International Group was giving me another opportunity to immerse myself with the local cultures in different Brazilian cities.

From Reno, Nevada, where my car was parked, I drove to Phoenix, Arizona. A group of ambassadors from India would join us in Brazil. Yes, it is true. I returned to living in my head and forgetting, on a conscious level, the clearing of my past abuse. Yet, at the same time, my emotional level retained all the intensity of this clearing. Since I was not truly present to my current state of being, I found myself easily annoyed, frustrated, and sometimes lonely and anxious. What I didn't realize was that my true self was still open and vulnerable with limited ability to adapt. I would eventually become present to what I had experienced in Bali. But first I needed time to process and gel the experience within every cell of my body. Instead, in typical fashion, I was off to Brazil where I would have little time to myself with hardly any chance to journal feelings, receive massages, or take soothing baths to feel into my new self. That would come much later.

Rio de Janeiro is a pulsating destination with much to see and experience. We walked the beaches of Ipanema and Copacabana, and attended a soccer match (or football game, as they refer to it) at the Mercado, complete with fireworks in the stands. Not unlike parts of New York City, Rio de Janeiro's downtown is bustling with energy, shops, restaurants, and businesses. There was also a visit to the Corcovado Mountain and the statue of Christ the Redeemer, and a Favela or shantytown tour. The movie *City of God* best depicts the life and neighborhoods of a Favela. My fascination for this tour left me forever imprinted with the eclectic living arrangements of some of the poorest people in Brazil. The morning tour had been cancelled due to a police raid, so I felt very lucky not to miss the experience.

We stayed two nights at Iguazu Falls in Iguazu National Park. The preservation of the park's biodiversity in 400,000 million hectares of virgin forest is coordinated by Brazil and Argentina. Four of us hired a taxi to take us to the more spectacular Argentina side of the falls. Since I had traveled quite a distance, I wanted to see as much as possible. We taxied as far as the farmers' blockade, which was protesting further government control.

Having to turn around and return to Brazil was a disappointment. At the same time my heart went out to people around the world who are hijacked by their governments, all in the name of wealth for a few individuals. Had we crossed the blockade, we might have missed our flight to Blumenau and our first homestay with the Friendship Force of Brazil. Blumenau is the central point of the German presence in Santa Catarina. Brazil has preserved the German settlers' culture and way of being. We were treated royally by this Friendship Force International Group.

Jair, Dilma, and their family greeted me after our flight and three-hour bus ride to their little Germantown. By now it was dark, so I was delighted the next morning by the view as we drove to connect with the rest of the group. We spent our days touring the city. We visited glass and textile factories, the Camboriu Beach, took a cable car ride to Unipraias Park, in addition to many other cultural events and dining delights. Several of the hardier members of the group biked to Recanto Silvestre, where we came together to bask in nature and eat an exquisitely catered lunch in the park pavilion.

Our second homestay required another flight, this time to Belo Horizonte, one of the larger cities in Brazil. Here I stayed with the chapter's president, Maria Clea Borges, in her downtown apartment. It felt so much like a New York City experience, which I loved. As a host, Maria was accommodating, sweet, and lovely to spend time with, and my homestay was extremely delightful. We spent the second week walking the town, attending cultural events, eating local foods, and celebrating my fifty-sixth birthday at Eni Granda Country House. We were actually enjoying home-cooked Brazilian foods, Capairinas (a fruity cocktail), songs, and country living—and I just happened to have my birthday. The Belo Horizonte Friendship Force group went all out for our exchange group, which represented several U.S. states and three members from India.

As the ambassador group boarded the plane to return to the United States and India, I flew to the Brazilian capital, Brasilia. I wanted to meet up with my friends Tiago and Livia, whom I had met at Esalen Institute. They were running Spa Zen Arte Vivenda Retreat Center and had invited me to visit with them. As always, my Brazilian flight served their staple, a warm ham and cheese sandwich. Not knowing when I would eat again, I ate the sandwich. Tiago picked me up at the airport and escorted me to my very own exquisite bungalow. At approximately two in the morning, I knew something was wrong. I made it to the bathroom just in time to expel every ounce of anything that was in my body through every possible portal. This continued for hours until I had no idea where in my body there could be anything left to expel. I found myself bungalow bound for three days, eating crackers and drinking the tea my friends brought me to soothe my stomach.

By the end of the third day, and still experiencing a wrenching gut, Tiago took me to a hospital. The doctor informed me there was nothing wrong with my lab tests and I could be on my way. I guess it doesn't look good for a foreign tourist to get food poisoning while in Brazil. I spent the remainder of the day, and the next two days, in a hammock on the porch of my bungalow watching Toucans in the trees. Tiago and Livia brought me fresh coconut water, tea, and crackers. I finally garnered the strength to wander this splendid piece of property with Zen gardens and caged birds that were being protected from extinction. This couldn't have happened at a better time or place on my trip.

All over Brazil, private homes are protecting scarlet macaws, blue and yellow macaws, and other endangered birds by keeping them caged. Poachers trap the birds and export them as exotic pets to countries such as ours. Thank you to these amazing individuals for all you do to allow these birds to live peacefully. Unfortunately, they are not thriving shut up in cages. Would education help reduce this tragedy created by human greed?

Tiago and Livia used their connections to link me with housing, drivers, and tour guides for my trip to Alto Paraiso de Goias. This little town in the mountains of Brazil afforded me an opportunity to travel by myself, even though I did not speak Portuguese. My tour guide, a friend of Livia's, met me at the bus and Tiago made sure I boarded safely. Our first stop was at an acai stand, a healthy treat of dark purple berries known in Brazil long before it was popular in the United States. Eating acai with granola set well on my stomach, which had just been wreaked upon by havoc.

My days in Alto Paraiso were sweet. If I didn't prepare a meal in my bungalow, I would eat at the local expat restaurant called Oca Lila. It was an easy place to make friends, and sometimes I ate alone on the rear deck. I didn't mind the walk to the restaurant for it afforded me the opportunity to view the toucans and parakeets flying freely.

Milena, my tour guide, would pick me up some days to take me into Chapada dos Veadeiros National Park. She shared with me one of the parks sweet spots, Vale Da Luna, with its rock formations formed into mysterious shapes by the rushing water. Well trained in Watsu, Jeanina Subriate gave me my first Watsu massage in a warm water pool in these mountains. The catharsis of Watsu left me relaxed, warm, and invigorated all at the same time. For the first time since returning from Bali, I was drawn back into my physical body, and this water therapy provided me with a flow to return to my emotional body once again. I did not need trauma to work on healing myself anymore. This was transformation time.

At the end of a peaceful day, we would often get together at a local pizza restaurant. Brazil has the best pizza I have ever tasted. On my last night in Alto Paraiso, we went to an outdoor restaurant where the pizza was baked in an open-air oven. Yum! The best part was the dessert pizza with chocolate and strawberries. The following day I would be traveling to visit John of God at his Casa de Dom Inacio in the town of Abadiania, Brazil. I still didn't speak Portuguese, so one of my friends wrote a note to tell the bus driver where to drop me off. This was a godsend for me. I was looking forward to Abadiania's inward focus and healing through meditation. I also anticipated with bated breath the powerful mediumship of Joao de Deus. Still, I will always remember Alto Paraiso with a warm heart.

By the time the bus arrived in the town of Abadiania, it was dark. The driver was not able to drop me off at the regular bus stop due to unattended brush fires blazing on the side of the road. When I got off the bus, I had no idea where the Casa was. My son, Tom, had told me that if I wanted to communicate in a foreign country, approaching youth was a solid choice. Schools around the world were teaching English, which forty-to-sixty-year-olds did not learn. I spotted a young couple sitting on a nearby porch. Once again, I thought, the Universe is conspiring with me. I was feeling grateful—and a little spoiled—that my native language was taught all over the world.

As it turned out, the young lovers did speak English, and the girl's father just happened to drive a taxi. He took me to the Dom Ingrid where I checked into a typical pousada, or hotel room, with stone walls, and doors that rattled and banged whenever someone closed them. Fortunately, the pousada was not overflowing with guests. There was a lot less door slamming than during the Casa's busy season.

I quickly learned where expat food was served and chose to eat my meals outside the pousada. Funny thing, I was picky with the food I put into my body, but given the chance, I sought out any available sweets. My favorite travel foods were pancakes with organic maple syrup or bread in any form: pizza, toast, sandwiches, calzones, sweet rolls. It would be some time before I acknowledged I was pacifying myself with food. My weight stretched and contracted like a rubber band. I could guess with accuracy how much I weighed just by the food I ate and the exercise I took.

Joao de Deus or Medium Joao Teixeira de Faria or John of God, as he is known internationally, is one of the world's prominent healers. He fulfills his physical and spiritual healings, or visible and invisible healings, at the Casa de Dom Inacio. Typically, I was a doubting Thomas when it came to the possibility of energy healing the physical, emotional, or spiritual imbalances from life's journeys. Since I was learning to receive love and healing in all its forms, when my doubting Thomas showed up, I thanked it and I remained open to all that is.

I would sit in "current" as they call it, or in a medium room with cleansing participants awaiting their experience with one of the thirty-three entities or spirits. An entity is a benevolent and advanced spirit who incorporates in John of God's body to heal the masses who visit the Casa each year. Joao does not take credit for the healings but rather says he is an instrument in God's divine hands, or an unconscious healer. It is all about intention and wanting to be healed, and I so wanted to be completely healed and whole again.

On my third day at the Casa, I was scheduled for a spiritual healing in the Intervention Room in front of the entity. I was instructed to take a taxi back to my posada—approximately 5,000 feet from the Casa—immediately and nurture myself for twenty-four hours as if I had had surgery. I was not to exercise, dance, or walk in public. I was just to rest. Someone from the Casa would bring me soup imbued with the energy from the entities so I could nourish myself, as everyone traveling to the Casa does.

Alone in my tiny room for a whole day, I started to crave my usual healthy, delicious dinner from the nearby café. After all, a person has to eat. What could a quick ten minutes out of my room do to me? I walked the 500 feet from my posada to the café, avoiding contact with people. I ordered my lunch, paid with exact change, and hurried back to my room to eat.

It wasn't long before I became aware of what actually had occurred while I stood in front of Joao imbued with an entity. My body shook for the next two hours as though my physical, emotional, and spiritual bodies were opened wide through surgery. Not following the Casa guidelines exposed me to incredible energy that my body could not transmute. I am now a believer. Something very powerful happens in the moment an entity heals. I do believe we can heal ourselves, and we can be healed as we open to other sources of healing energy such as John of God. For six weeks, I found myself not needing to use a sleep apnea dental device or a CPAP machine to correct my sleep apnea. How sweet it was.

I stayed in Abadiania for two additional days pondering the power of spirit and talking with other people from all over the world who had come to the Casa for healing. I am not sure what else to say other than my recommendation is to go to Brazil and experience John of God for yourself. He also travels to the United States once a year to allow entities to perform healings at places such as Omega Institute in New York. Joao de Deus says, "I do not heal anyone, the one who heals is God."

Returning to Spa Zen in Brasilia for my final night in Brazil, I reconnected with my friends Tiago and Livia, giving me a chance to acknowledge them for nursing me to health again. I treated them to an all-you-can-eat pizza dinner in downtown Brasilia. My favorite is still the chocolate and strawberries dessert pizza. All-you-can-eat pizza dinners are about as pricey as a nice meal in a big American city. Afterward, the three of us went sightseeing. A highlight was the Catedral Metropolitana, a landmark cathedral by award-winning architect Oscar Niemeyer. It was bittersweet saying good-bye to such wonderful friends and my adventure-filled time in Brazil.

On the plane to Miami, I passed on the ham and cheese sandwich and ate my own food instead. During the flight, I processed a lot that had occurred for me in Brazil and Bali. My heart was wide-open to the people of both countries who had shared their lives and nurtured me in my physical and emotional pain.

By this point in 2008, I had been out of the United States more than I was in it. It felt good to step on my motherland soil and hug the familiar, loving face of my sister Lauren before setting off for Ecuador and the Amazon. The box of supplies I had sent for my next trip had arrived. I spent a few days with Lauren and her family before continuing my intense journey. That also gave me time to sort through my belongings and ship items I wouldn't need for Ecuador to my friend Carol in Cleveland. Thank goodness for Lauren and Carol. I felt love on all sides.

Following the intensity of Bali and Brazil, spending time on native soil turned out to be a good choice. It gave me a reprieve from going deeply into my past and processing the various issues that had bubbled up for me, especially in Bali. I played with my nephew, Blake, by the pool, took a trip into the Everglades, and visited with my sister Rose and her husband, who live in the Tampa, Florida, area. I had not seen Rose in several years and it was a heartwarming reunion. My last two days in Florida were spent unpacking, packing, shipping, and saying good-bye again.

CHAPTER 12

Unattached to the Outcome

(Ecuador)

*"I've seen miracles in post-war
situations, in famines, in places of
horrendous brutal subjugation and
oppression, when women step forward
and play their rightful role in co-equal
partnership with men. It's not the
answer all by itself, but it is a
powerful and incredibly effective step
to give women their rightful role and
voice and the resources to back it up."*
—LYNNE TWIST

While at Esalen Institute, my friend Pauline suggested that I look into a trip to Ecuador with the Pachamama Alliance. It took several conversations with Pauline before I explored their website, but once I did I was sold on the trip into Achuar territory. By then the trip was fully booked, and I was placed on a waiting list. Again the Universe conspired with me for my higher good. While in Bali, I received an email from The Pachamama Alliance that a space had opened up and could I get a substantial deposit to them within a week. Because I wouldn't be returning to the States for another five weeks, and since sharing my charge card number on a long distance call or on email was not secure, I was on a mission to figure out an alternative method of payment.

Did I say the Universe conspired with me? A new friend from Texas, whom I had met in a dance class in Bali, was returning to the States in three days. Fortunately, I had extra cash and travelers checks on my trip to Bali and would be fine financially for five more weeks. She agreed to take $500 cash with her, write a check to TPA, and voila! I would be going to Ecuador. The Universe had trusted that this trip was for me to do at this time in my life, and I trusted my friend with my money.

I had written curriculum in Bali, traveled for six weeks in Brazil, visited family in Florida, and like a whirlwind I now flew to Ecuador. Quito, the capital of Ecuador, had grown up around the airport, thus flights land literally in the center of the city. In this struggling country, moving the airport to safer environs was a financial challenge. At the same time, everything about Quito was crowded, exciting, and a delight for adventurous Carolyn.

Due to three months of intense travel, I knew very little about what my Ecuador experience might entail. On the second evening, the rainforest journey started with a group meeting led by David Tucker, the Pachamama Journeys director. David had been holding conference calls with the group for several months. The organization's mission is to deliver experiences designed to educate and inspire individuals everywhere to bring forth a thriving, just, and sustainable world. They have a knowing that we can transform human systems and structures that keep us separate, thus becoming each other's strongest allies in ensuring a vibrant future. Everything about this mission resonated with me. The Pachamama Alliance staff communicated integrity and passion about possibilities. The group was honored to meet Lynne Twist, one of the co-founders of The Pachamama Alliance this evening before our immersion into the rainforest. It doesn't get any better than that. They so inspired me to want to make a difference for all life on this planet.

I knew from this meeting that I would want to be in a flow state: changing from operating out of my head to a heart-centered strategy in order to adapt to my coming experience. I was still feeling a little emotionally bankrupt from my breakdown in Bali and the intensity of the spiritual healing in Brazil. Once again, I questioned why I chose to go on another profound trip, and I was frightened.

There really wasn't anything to fear. I was learning to trust the wisdom of my physical being. I would stay in the wonderment and listen to the emotions and sensations of my heart and body. My feelings were still circulating, following my opening in Bali, and this was helping me to decipher good from not-good situations before they occurred. Healthy functioning was all new to me. I would put a bubble around me, not as armor but as a raincoat or a sort of membrane. I didn't want to be controlled by my fear. I was keenly aware that what I feared would come into my life. After all, FEAR is False Emotions Appearing Real, and I would honor and trust the wisdom of my soul. My soul had once left me through abuse but had returned so I could love who I was, at the soul level. This trip was opening a new door for me.

At our evening meeting, our Pachamama guide, David Tucker reiterated what was suggested in our pre-trip telephone meetings, "Pay attention to and honor your dreams." In a mere two days, we met our Achuar guide at Kapawi Eco Lodge deep in the Achuar territory of the Ecuadorian rainforest. The Achuar are one of the world's most intact indigenous civilizations. They are a dream culture. They awaken at 4:00 A.M. every morning and tell their dreams around the fire. From this sharing, the elders decide what they will do in life that day. They live their dreams in a powerful way and we were to do the same.

Flying into the Amazon on a six-seater plane required strict adherence to weight requirements. We left the majority of our belongings behind and took only our basic necessities, including biodegradable products. The Achuar use only what they need and give back equally to Mother Earth. We would do the same.

Our journey to the town of Shell was prefaced by a visit with a Quechua shaman high in the Andes. The shaman cleansed us of any negative residue in preparation for our journey deep into the 2,000,000 acres of pristine primary forests in Achuar territory.

David encouraged us to journal and provided group processing circles each evening. We quickly began to connect by sharing our intimate experiences with nature, our dreams, and the people of Ecuador. There was an air of nonjudgment, openness, and compassion that I attributed to the grounded individuals in the group, despite the broad range of ages: seventeen through sixty-five. David's presence alone explained why he leads trips into the Amazon rainforest in the Achuar territory of Ecuador. This was a partnership by invitation from the Achuar in order to expand their base of allies supporting the preservation of their ancient culture and pristine rainforest, upon which all life depends. People who choose to immerse themselves in this partnership care deeply for Mother Nature, thus my immersion was a no-brainer.

The Achuar have managed to preserve this crucial part of our world while their neighbors' land and way of being have been destroyed. Other nations harvest the Amazon's natural resources, such as trees and oil, so the developed world can continue to consume most of the Earth's resources. Now, in partnership with The Pachamama Alliance, the Achuar are lobbying on behalf of the natural world. They have learned Spanish, and some have gone on to learn English through their own organization, Fundacion Pachamama. The Achuar are keepers of the rainforest.

With Kapawi Lodge as our home base, our Achuar guides took us in dugout canoes, on foot, and sometimes in covered river boats further into the rainforest. We hiked through the Amazon in boots up to our knees and floated down the Pastaza River watching monkeys, macaws, and the renowned pink dolphins. Our day might begin at 3:00 A.M., joining an Achuar community to process our dreams with the elders and shamans. Most days, we interacted with the local people, plants, and animals and learned about the Achuar culture and traditional foods and crafts.

At the end of the day, I rested in a hammock, gazing out at the hummingbirds and egrets in the lagoon. This provided the perfect setting to process all that had occurred. Sinking into the beauty of our Earth's lungs, and knowing the human species would not survive without the rainforest, created pause for future activation. Later in the evening, falling asleep to the sounds of the nocturnal creatures assured me of deep dreaming about what is possible for our Earth. Offering blessings to roadkill no longer seemed odd to me. I am so thankful for all the beings on Earth who provide a richness in which my life can thrive. I become overwrought when a piece of the whole is destroyed, whether roadkill or the richness of the lungs of the Earth.

The most wide-reaching highlight of my rainforest trip was the multiple overnights in an Achuar village. Deeper in the Amazon, tents were pitched and we immersed ourselves in a culture of autonomous people. We attended a graduation party in the local one-room schoolhouse, harvested cassava, and replanted the roots with the women while the men crafted blow darts. We watched the woman of the house make the drink chicha while other women created pottery and painted identifying symbols on the bowls. We shared songs and dances with each other. The Northerners chose the Hokey Pokey never considering that "We put our backside in and shake it all about" might be offensive to another culture. However, we all laughed, including the Achuar.

The program provided many opportunities to drink chicha, eat slugs, and meet the elders and shamans. Chicha is the only beverage the Achuar drink, including the children. They never drink water. This drink of choice has a spiritual component. The cassava is cooked over the fire and only the women can touch it. They pull large pieces out of the family pot with their fingers then chew the mixture to blend it, just as we would do with a blender. They then spit it back into the pot, allowing it to ferment till it's ready to drink. Joining in the ceremony, we would all gather around drinking chicha while the elders talked. The Ecuadorian guides interpreted what was said and David would clarify it for us.

After several intense months at Esalen, in Bali, and in Brazil, I was ripe to undergo a shift. And I was truly experiencing an inner and an outer shift. I realized at a deep level that when I die, I want to be remembered not for what I have accumulated or for what I know but for how my life has made a difference for my fellow human beings.

I had not been aware that my beliefs were based on what I had learned growing up, living as a white, privileged, Catholic female with many years of education. I was all about what I was taught, had heard, what I'd experienced, and it was slanted. I had moved toward a survivor's temperament. Now I was taking ownership of my experiences as a mirror of myself and beginning to find ways to step into who I was becoming. I learned to stand in my own power as I redeemed myself.

You might ask how I could be privileged having gone through an abusive childhood, sleeping in my closet where I felt protected. We are all connected through our challenges and our solutions. If we are all connected and are all mirrors of each other, then judgment will always dampen the soul. I was learning that I was what was in my soul not what I had experienced. I was now choosing to live with grace, peace, and love.

Clarity about the rainforest being an integral part of my shift was important to my becoming who I was meant to be. The shift occurred on my Pachamama Alliance trip in the rainforest with the Achuar. It wouldn't have been so profound had I not done "my work" at Esalen, in Bali, and in Brazil and with Jaclyn, my therapist. Clearing out the heavy baggage opened me to new and exciting possibilities for the future. I can't deny my experiences. They happened. But now my hero's compassion for myself was kicking in to tell me, "I am enough."

I was high on life and inspired to make a difference. I had a new sense of self after my journey of the previous six months. The inspiration I found from the Achuar and The Pachamama Alliance, coupled with seeing the vast devastation of the western slope of the Rocky Mountains, the deforestation of the redwoods in California, and the pollution of Lake Erie, to name a few, was being felt deep within my soul. Then, seeing piles of garbage in developing countries such as Uganda, rivers polluted with plastic bags and bottles as in Bali, and learning about the great swirl of trash in the Pacific Ocean created a layer of sadness and grief for Mother Earth. I no longer felt the grief of my past, for it had been cleared. I sensed the urgency to make a difference on behalf of all life on this planet.

PART V

Connection

(pictured on previous page) Feeling the energy of the Great Kapok tree in the Ecuadorian Amazon is a magical experience. The beauty and majesty of this canopy provides shade from the hot sun and the soft gentle rain.

CHAPTER 13

We Are All Connected

"There is a field of energy that connects
all of creation."
—GREGG BRADEN

Returning to the United States gave me the opportunity to pick a home, since I no longer had one. My body was longing for rest, integration, and an abode with stability, familiarity, and quietness. Through a Yahoo group email, I connected with Chris, who was returning to Costa Rica for three months, and sublet his apartment in Boulder complete with a full set of dishes, silverware, pots and pans, and my very own bathroom. I had a living room with a large screen television and a washer and dryer. The first thing I did was wash every piece of clothing that had sat in the suitcases in my car for more than six months. I was cleansing the last bit of my journey in preparation for my new life.

Next, I researched where the closest Awakening the Dreamer Symposium was. This signature program of The Pachamama Alliance is usually attended by individuals prior to traveling into the Amazon.

Not me. I barely knew who or what The Pachamama Alliance was before arriving at Kapawi Lodge in the Amazon. In fact, having little time to research and immerse myself in the program, I just opened to the possibilities and stayed unattached to the outcome of my rainforest journey. What I came to realize about this trip is that it touched my heart deeply and forever changed my life.

In Boulder, there were symposiums in several venues. After attending one close to where I was living, my heart opened wide. I knew this was not a coincidence. A training for participants who wanted to facilitate this program was scheduled five minutes from where I was living. I registered knowing this was what I would do to make a difference. Again, this was not a coincidence.

Just as my rainforest trip was transformative, the Awakening the Dreamer Facilitator Training was equally life changing. An incredible group of forty-three potential facilitators, three training leaders, and a support team of many committed individuals spent four full days together learning, connecting, and exploring ways to awaken others to the urgency of bringing about a sustainable and just human presence for all life on Mother Earth.

Having paid little attention to world news and not having watched television (even in hotel rooms) for four years, I realized I had allowed myself to be removed from the collective madness of the third dimension. During my training to be a facilitator, I became aware that a portion of the shift in me was also a shift in humanity. There was a spiral of evolution occurring that quickly increased my awareness and uplifted my heart. I began to acknowledge that if I wasn't speaking from my heart, I was not living from my heart. This phenomenon of living from the heart and *stepping out* was happening all over the world. Paul Hawken says, "There is another super power here on earth that is an unnamed movement. It is far different and bigger and more unique than anything we have ever seen. It flies under the radar of the media by and large." People were *stepping up* all over this planet to make a difference and I had been oblivious to it.

I came to Earth to live a life of love. In fact, we all came to Earth to love. It is what life is all about. The heart connects the mind and body and expands the self to include others. It's all about connection and love, and we are all connected. Science has proven our interconnectedness and describes it through mirror neurons in the brain. When we see someone else perform a deed or emote, our mirror neurons are activated in the exact same way. Mirror neurons provide a powerful basis for the evolution of culture. We are part of a larger whole with no separation between ourselves and other global human beings. Your success is my success. My failures are your failures. Your healing is my healing. It is all of us or none of us. We will unite and honor all ways of all races in order to survive. The challenges we face are huge. The Evolutionary Shift occurring on our planet now will bring about a new way to be, and together we are a genius.

CHAPTER 14

Mirrors

"Every tree and plant in the meadow
seemed to be dancing, those with
average eyes see
as fixed and still."
—MOWLAVI

There is another way to be. Everyone loses when things are not fair. I was learning about unconditional love and restoring balance not only to myself but to everyone I came in contact with. I had a long way to go. I would listen each day to what I was grateful for and what had touched my heart. As I learned to change my focus, I began to see there was another way to be.

If everything is a mirror of myself, then judgment and anger toward another are really judgment and anger that needs to heal in myself. I don't need or want to feel guilty, so letting go of the shoulds, coulds, and woulds opens up new possibilities. I can change my perception of other people, thus creating a situation in which others show up differently, thus changing how I think of them. My data had been running me in this universal consciousness. Since people are mirrors of myself, changing the perception of the data presented a whole new picture in the mirror. Now, I can be compassionate toward other human beings who have made different choices than I have made. I can look at myself and ask, "What part of me has hurt others in a similar way?" I don't want to ignore my human weaknesses but acknowledge them, love them, and forgive myself when I forget who I truly am. There is so much more to us than I had ever acknowledged.

We are programmed to help others and to share. You make a difference and I make a difference. Mother Teresa said, "There is more hunger for love and appreciation in this world than for bread." It is often said that we need four hugs a day for survival, eight hugs for maintenance, and twelve for growth. As I return closer to the source of who I really am, I authentically interact with others, seeing the incredible human beings that they are, and offer hugs along the way. What I experience is that people "show up" in my life as I envision them. By staying open to this tenet in my life, I also note that there is always free will. With that said, I know the importance of remembering that compassion is the absence of judgment. Those I have forgiven with love may continue to act in ways that are contrary to my way.

My new awakening puts me on a higher level of responsibility to my global family. It gives my heart pause as I live in a state of forgiveness with clarity and compassion. I am always looking for evidence of love and gratitude in my life.

CHAPTER 15

Being With All That Is

"Yesterday we obeyed kings and bent
our necks before emperors. But, today,
we kneel only to truth, follow only
beauty, and obey only love."
—KAHLIL GIBRAN

The world is changing rapidly. When I left on my journey, smart phones, Facebook, and Twitter were just starting to become mainstream, and mostly for twenty- and thirty-somethings. When I ended my travels four years later, I was on Facebook and LinkedIn, and was organizing groups and folders in my email with nearly a thousand contacts. This is eight hundred more than when I had left. I soon became aware that the world was evolving—and quickly.

Beginning my journey around the world saw me sitting on a telephone landline to make flight and hotel reservations. I had purchased only a few items on the Internet and did not give my charge card number over a cell phone. At the end of four years, I was using a smart phone and purchasing just about everything on the Internet.

Scheduling deliveries was a balancing act because I was seldom in one place for very long. My accounts and bills were paid via the Internet out of necessity, since I did not get my mail more than a half-dozen times a year. My commercial habits changed along with the world. It was similar to an idea whose time had come. As Deepak Chopra says, "Instead of thinking outside the box, get rid of the box." I had gotten rid of many boxes that were keeping me from growing.

Even though I was open to all that was evolving and changing in the world and seeing the possibilities, my experience of living life in a big way would not come to complete fruition for another year. Just as the caterpillar does not experience new growth until the old is shed, I was continuing to shed my old self, which was not dead but merely in a state of evolution along with my world family. Slowly my irritability faded away as my sense of self returned. Mohandas Gandhi said, "As human beings, our greatness lies not so much in being able to remake the world as in being able to remake ourselves." I was immersed in the throes of remaking myself. The metamorphosis of my chrysalis into a butterfly would come more slowly than I had cared to think.

I was satisfied with my travels and ready to root and live in one place. That was when I took a 350-square-foot apartment in Boulder. I wanted and intended to wake up each day full of energy and a joy for living. Most days, that was not the case. My sleep apnea was sounding its siren at 5,430 feet above sea level and my current sleep apnea dental device was no longer stopping the apneas. I discovered also that I was B12 deficient once again and my thyroid medication needed to be tweaked. I seemed to be challenged by things that made me tired. I was frustrated with wanting to step into my new self while being countered by my body screaming for sleep.

If the ultimate expression of health is a person's ability to adapt, I was very unhealthy. My deficient adaptation to my new apartment was shown through my physical lethargy, mental forgetfulness, and inability to socially integrate and sort through the multiple spiritual modalities I had come upon while traveling. There seemed to be a sense of separation from self. The many blood tests to balance my thyroid, exploring the use of a B12 patch behind my ear instead of a weekly injection, and returning to a CPAP machine for my sleep apnea left me wanting to accept what was. I had exercised wanderlust and now it was integration time.

I thanked the sleep apnea for showing up in my life to give me time to step back and rest my weary body. I developed a daily practice of yoga, meditation, hiking, and biking, and expanded the variety of foods I was eating and buying, mostly organic, to reduce my body's exposure to toxins. Many days, I remained at home so as not to push myself to exhaustion. I danced to music from Esalen, took warm sea salt baths, and practiced breathing exercises.

All in all, meditation was the powerful influence that helped me go inside to find what was mine to do at this time in history. The noise of the world was as loud as my chattering monkey mind. Getting quiet allowed my soul's whisper to be heard. Einstein said, "No problem can be solved from the same level of consciousness that created it." Having traveled the world, my eyes were opened and I began to see. I was getting off the treadmill of unexamined assumptions about how my way of living affected my fellow human beings. Every purchase became a conscious choice. Through mindfulness meditation, I was paying attention to the present moment and knew we are all being called into greatness. Meditation helped me to see that my ancestors were calling, and I was picking up the phone.

Traveling around the world was not the only thing that created my transformation from survivor of abuse to woman in action. Staying unattached to the outcome with each experience, and remaining vulnerable to memories and emotions that surfaced, aided my growth. My unconsciousness to be free of my past became conscious as I paid attention to what was coming up for me. Dr. Rohini Kanniganti says, "Challenge without resources equals stress and challenges with resources equals resilience." I learned to access resources and face the challenges along the way. I was willing to do whatever it took to detach from what was holding me down. "You can cage the singer but not the song," said Harry Belafonte. I was caged with my song inside most of my life. My journey helped me to break free, sing my song, and make a difference for all life on this planet. I knew life had no remote. I would need to step up, step out, and change it myself.

There are infinite pathways to penetrating our core being to expose what is stopping us from being the person we were meant to be. I chose the therapy route then meshed it with Gestalt, the movement arts, journaling, meditation, and other healing modalities. I knew I was clearing my past when memories appeared in my life with a lessened emotional charge. Today, I remain active through hiking, biking, skiing, and yoga, as well as advancing my well-being through Donald Epstein's Network Spinal Analysis and Somato Respiratory Integration. Both modalities assist me in living an exhilarating and healthy life. I know I have peeled most of the onion layers when the memories appear in my life with a lessened emotional charge. The clearing continues today at a different level. Ralph Waldo Emerson said, "Life is a journey, not a destination."

A personal example I can share goes like this...I recently was attending a book study group that had a chapter about doing our personal work and living in a world numb to emotions. In order for us to be present to our bodies, expressing emotions in a healthy manner is essential. Only then can we step into our greatness. This chapter led me to share my story with members who knew nothing of my past. I was present to the fact that as I told the story, I did not clear my throat, start shaking inside, or stare at the ceiling. I was present to the group; the telling about my past was matter of fact. The story no longer elicited strong emotions. I was connected to my feelings rather than feeling numb and controlled by them.

I would like to say to you, as the world continues to evolve, we want to be ready through having done our personal work. The huge mansions in this country will become community houses. Living with others will be a necessity requiring new ways to be. We are moving toward a more sustainable way of life where everyone gets what they need, not necessarily all they want. We are all connected. We are all one. The choices I make minute by minute impact my seven billion brothers and sisters on this planet. Whatever I do to you, I do to myself, my family, and my children. When we truly identify with this concept of one, living in community will be easier.

Doing our personal work on what has us caged is crucial for humans to live productively in community. Our personal work creates the clearing needed to stand compassionately in our power, not to defend our actions of integrity, but to state boundaries and be open to staying in the conversation until an issue is resolved. I know that expressing emotions, contributing fairly, picking up the slack for someone in crisis, choosing kindness over righteousness, and stepping up and sharing my gifts is part of the new paradigm happening now. All this and more will create a space for a healthy community to exist in the new paradigm—a more just and sustainable way to be.

What is your path to having the most meaningful life you can have? Listen to your feelings. If another person triggers strong negative emotions, that's a sign there is work to be done. An acquaintance stopped talking with me mid-sentence once and walked away. I could have said, "What a jerk! Who the heck do they think they are?" Instead, I chose, "I didn't say or do anything to cause them to walk away." Then and only then, I could look at what emotions came up for me, look into my past when I felt like this before, perhaps when an elder rejected me when I was seven, then examine what in me wanted to be healed. I find this approach keeps me on the path of clearing of issues, holding my head up high, and living in a state of non-judgment. If I realize I am still hurting from this incident when I was seven and want to clear it, I journal, dance, talk with a therapist, or drum about it. It then may be cleared enough for me to forgive them and, most importantly, forgive my seven-year-old self. I am valuable just the way I am. I realize now that the journey to wholeness is ongoing. It is a process, not a destination.

Just how deep the wound is may indicate how much clearing needs to happen. Sometimes it may seem as though it is cleared, then it shows its face again at another present-day rejection. Each time it surfaces, it becomes less of a trigger, with a smaller charge. Set your intention to clear until you can be around people who previously triggered you. Choose to say, "It just isn't that big of a deal anymore," and feel it in your heart because you have done your work. Then you know you are making progress on your journey to clear all the baggage from your past. We can live a healthy, peaceful, meaningful life with other human beings. It is possible and so worth it.

What did I learn on my four-year journey?

- Writing in a gratitude journal each day for just a few minutes refocuses my perception that it isn't all bad. There are things to be grateful for. Feelings of gratitude are a sign of wholeness.
- It is not all about having what I want, but wanting what I have.
- Fairness is everyone getting what they need, not necessarily what they want.
- Holding a grudge is letting someone live rent-free in my head.
- If I keep replaying the last chapter of my life, I can't start the next chapter. Clearing the last chapter opens huge possibilities for the future. Ignoring the last chapter will manifest in an unhealthy way.
- Restoring balance requires me to be in the discomfort of the unpleasant feelings that arise when I go deeply into the wounds of the past.
- Negative feelings, such as anger, are smoke alarms alerting me to past injuries that I can clear and be free from.
- A traumatized self is an unconscious self. Becoming conscious of past injuries can create a boldness to heal, discover, and imagine a whole new way to be.
- When I became tired of being a victim, I accepted reality with a fierce truthfulness about what happened in my life and did not cower in fear. I experienced the moment without analyzing or blaming.

- There is majesty in healing. Part of healing is in forgiveness of others and, more importantly, forgiveness of myself. I love the ancient Hawaiian practice of reconciliation and forgiveness called Ho'oponopono: I am sorry. Please forgive me. I love you. Thank you.

- There is no separation between ourselves and our global family. What we do to ourselves, we do to each other.

- I want to give up complaining and blaming, to choose to accept and be open to possibilities.

- By seeing the hope and possibility, I have the option of being in love, joy, and bliss and staying in my heart, unattached to the outcome. By staying unattached to the outcome, I can set intentions that are pure and can beget a gentle and pure outcome.

- When I am determined, I stop loving what I do and grit my teeth all the way. I want to be gentle, soft, kind, and love everything I do.

- Every thought I think and every word I say creates my reality.

- Femininity is like a swaying willow tree in a storm. It is gentle. It is not like a maple tree that cracks.

- Instead of going into my cave, it is okay to allow others to nurture me in times of challenge.

- Rather than getting stuck in group energy, I can choose to be my own person with my own ideas and actions.

- I won't get to where I want to go in the growth arena by logic.

- Opening to my heart, feeling my feelings, listening, and being present to what is showing up in my life as messages from the Universe rather than coincidences, will show me possibilities I may not have seen on my own.

- Following what presents itself is more important than what might appear logical in my limited view.

- Without holding on to others' feelings as my own, I can feel their feelings and then let the feeling flow back to them, so as to be compassionate rather than sympathetic.

- Being my own person in a relationship is crucial, for if the relationship ends, I will be okay because I will have a strong sense of myself and who I am.

- It is okay to ask for assistance. I don't have to do everything myself.
- It is good to surround myself with people who believe in my dreams.
- Helping others is healthy when I come from a place of service without control, rather than a place of need for recognition.
- Checking inside for my motivation in doing anything is crucial, thus asking myself, "What is my intention for doing this?" Then, if it is in alignment with my values, I will continue. If not, I reevaluate my direction.
- One path in life may be easier to take; the other path may be more satisfying.
- I can break out of the fear of what others may think and surge forward with the integrity and strength of who I am being.
- The Universe and my body are the same. Trees are my lungs and water is my blood. We are all one.
- Integrity is about authenticity in keeping agreements and taking responsibility for myself.
- To heal an injury, I must recognize the injury, own the injury, understand it, forgive my perpetrators, forgive myself, release the injury with appreciation and all that goes with it, and replace the injury with a positive experience.
- I know that I can choose to stay in a place of feeling angry, or I can choose to transmute the anger and replace it with a positive feeling by following the steps listed above.
- No feelings are bad. I can have a feeling without judging the feeling and just accept it as it is.
- Kent Healy says, "Perception is not reality but it becomes reality when we believe only what we already know and disregard other possibilities in life."
- I am not my history. I am who I am becoming.

CHAPTER 16

Be a Caterpillar

*"Shining our light gives others the
permission
to shine theirs."*
—MARIANNE WILLIAMSON

*"It is a felony against universal law to
ignore inner guidance and not live
your purpose. It will actually lead to
illness and disease."*
—JACK CANFIELD

*"Tell me, what is it you plan to do
with your one wild and precious life?"*
—MARY OLIVER

Making the decision to sell my spacious, beautiful home and its contents to travel the world, it was as if I was appeasing my adventurous spirit. The truth was I was courageously immersing myself in every scenario crossing my path in order to clear what was stopping me from being who I was meant to be. I didn't realize the true purpose for leaving on my journey until I shed the physical attachments keeping me from being free, and walked into the fire.

As a result, I transformed my entire life rather than just some years of my life. I found myself, rather than a community to lean on or a man to take care of me. I now have friends all around the globe and a new way to view the world, her people, and other life beings. I have ascertained my deep value system, which I couldn't verbalize before. Listening deeply to my fellow human beings with compassion and nonjudgment is second nature to me now. I am clear about my teaching and facilitating gifts. I have identified that I am a connector of people, activities, and organizations.

For years I had been searching for who I really was in the world and what my purpose was. I wanted to know what life was all about. Freeing myself of the things that tied me down created a spaciousness for opportunities to appear, for me to grow and transform. After fifty-four years of crawling out of the cement vault surrounding my very being, I began to leap. I would never have guessed this was a possibility for my life.

The Black Swan Theory says that when something that is unpredictable and outside the realm of regular expectations occurs, it has a high impact on societies and is then explained as if it were predictable and expected. My transformation was unpredictable, and I intend to impact society with who I am being in 2012 and beyond. Yet I have no desire to explain my transformation in hindsight as if I or the world expected it. I explored, cleared past history, transformed, and it could not have been predicted. My journey is not in the realm of the Black Swan Theory, but I am a powerful force for change.

My impact on society is grounded in a more sustainable and just way to live, with a pledge to my children's children. With all that is at this time in history—the weather changes and cataclysmic storms, the financial and political power in the hands of a few, the seven billion human beings vying for their fair share of the limited resources of Mother Earth, the human enslavement and sex trade operations, the abuse of animals, the alteration of food leading to a minimal choice of healthy food in groceries around the world and especially in the United States—everyone needs to do their part. I want to know that my life made a difference when I die. I am guessing you do too.

I could go on and on and perhaps even write another book about sustainability and justice. I am choosing to wake people to what is true about this time we are living in. I want to support others in identifying what to do to live a meaningful life. My gift to the shift is teacher, facilitator, connector, and coach. In Cleveland, the Staying Awake Community at River's Edge is thriving and bringing the message of sustainability and justice to the masses. This community was a brainstorm of mine, and I spent a year and a half connecting with or-ganizations and like-minded people to create a group who truly understands what is possible at this time in history. Today, they continue to meet, evolve, and truly make a difference all over Northeast Ohio. Their primary tool is the Awakening the Dreamer Symposium.

I would like to invite you to explore my website, www.Carolyn-RoseHart.com, to inquire into the resources, programs, coaching and articles available to you. This website will continue to grow and evolve on a regular basis and contains my blog. Come blog with me.

So what do you need to do at this time in history? We all have a part to play to make a difference for all life on this planet. I believe, at a deep level, we all know this. Sometimes, as people enter a transition stage in their life, they wait and wait for what to do next. I am all about *stepping up* and *stepping out*. You have incredible gifts to share. Ask yourself:

- What are my gifts?
- Have I done my personal work for the collective evolution happening on our planet right now?

Sign-up on my website to receive your free "Guide to Identifying Your Gifts."

Personal work can occur simultaneously with our collective work. It can also occur singly, as in my journey, and evolve slowly as you step into the work that will make a difference for humanity. Likewise, personal work can occur in many other forms. At times, it may be necessary to clear past history through sessions with a therapist skilled in the components of your story. From my experience, the many sessions with Jaclyn became invaluable to my transformation. For others, deep movement, meditation, connection with nature, or sessions with a coach, etc., may suffice. I would like to invite you to start doing your personal work today. Each of us will do what is ours to do. Life is a dance floor and you are the music.

Jean Houston says, "There are evolutionary accelerators that propel us from beneath the surface crust of sleepy consciousness and our own human nature. To respond and become proactive in the mythic tasks that are now upon us, our basic nature is challenged to deepen, discover, and evolve."

Necessity is the mother of invention, and there is a need now for humanity to do things differently. The world needs people who have come alive. By embracing the challenges we face, life becomes full of exciting possibilities. Individuals can make money to support their lives, share their gifts, and do good all at the same time. *Stepping up* and *stepping out* invites the Universe to show us the way. As each of us generates ripples of change through who we are and what we do, magical things will happen. How will you show up?

About the Author

Carolyn Rose Hart is an educator who chose to follow her dream after completing thirty years of teaching challenged learners. She achieved a Master of Education degree plus sixty-seven hours, all while raising her two children as a single parent. Her growing passion for clearing the abuse in her life spurred exploration of other opportunities to go deeply into the pain. This questing inspired her to explore the U.S. and took her across the globe into Sub-Saharan Africa, Indonesia, and the Amazon. Working with master teachers and with techniques such as Gestalt, massage, dance, chanting, and connection with nature led her to soften and become an advocate for women and children.

Carolyn's leadership experience began long ago as a team leader, department chairperson, and team trainer. Since retiring from teaching, she has initiated the Uganda Teacher Fund and presented dozens of Awakening the Dreamer Symposiums (ATD). She now trains others to facilitate this program. The Staying Awake Community in Cleveland was her brainchild and she has become sort of the "Pachamama" of Cleveland. Inspiring others to *step up* and *step out* is part of her new American Dream. Carolyn is a giver of the nine Peruvian rites of the Munay Ki, rites of initiation to become an Earthkeeper.

In addition to *Step Up, Step Out: Share Your Gifts and Be an Agent for Change*, Carolyn is published in the anthology, *Pebbles in the Pond: Transforming the World One Person at a Time*. The Pebbles initiative was the brainchild of Christine Kloser, the Transformation Catalyst.

Carolyn currently explores all possibilities in writing and blogging with her worldwide community and maintains an active presence on LinkedIn, Facebook, and Twitter. She is an avid organizer, woman's collaborator, speaker, teacher, photographer, compassionate listener, and an author with a compelling story to share. Her new passion is coaching others to pinpoint what matters to them most in life through the identification of their gifts. Her love for Dances of Universal Peace, hiking, biking, skiing, and snowshoeing provides the balance in her life to live fully into her passion. Check out Carolyn's website and blog at www.CarolynRoseHart.com. Connect with her on Facebook at StepUpStepOutBook and Tweet with her at https://twitter.com/#!/StepupStepoutbk.

About the cover:

I personally took this photo following my immersion into the Achuar Territory in the Amazon at the end of my journey. I returned to my childhood home only to find it boarded up and in doing an internet search found it was scheduled for demolition. I could have gone into a place of sadness but instead saw the gift in this demolition. I had released the abuse that mainly occurred in this home and it was quite timely to release the house to the wrecking ball.

The book cover is a photo of the steps leading to the backyard and the back door of the house. The memories of my mother weeding the beautiful gardens on either side of the steps remains vibrant. These gardens no longer existed. It was her escape and connection with nature in her gardens that kept her alive for her children.

Manjari, my awesome book cover designer, helped me choose and formulate a personal photo that had meaning and vibrance for the cover of *Step Up Step Out*. Thank you, Manjari

Give the Gift of

Step Up, Step Out

Share Your Gifts and Be an Agent for Change to Your Friends and Colleagues

CHECK YOUR LEADING BOOKSTORE OR ORDER HERE.

YES, I want _____ copies of Step, Up, Step Out: Share Your Gifts and Be an Agent for Change at $14.95 each, plus $4.95 shipping per book (Boulder, Colorado, residents please add 1.23 sales tax per book). Canadian orders must be accompanied by a postal money order in U.S. funds. Allow 15 days for delivery.

YES, I am interested in having Carolyn Rose Hart speak or give a seminar to my company, association, school, or organization. Please send information.

My check or money order for $_____ is enclosed.

Name _____

Organization _____

Address _____

City/State/Zip _____

Phone _____

Email _____

Please make your check payable and return to:

Spiritwise Publishing
PO Box 93
Boulder , Colorado 80306http://carolynrosehart.com/